I0411782

What makes Superman a hero is not that he has power, but that he has the wisdom and the maturity to use the power wisely. From an acting point of view, that's how I approached the part.

Christopher Reeve

Singing is a way of releasing an emotion that you sometimes can't portray when you're acting. And music moves your soul, so music is the source of the most intense emotions you can feel. When you hear a song and you're acting it's incredible. But when you're singing a song and you're acting it's even more incredible.

Amanda Seyfried

There is a need for aloneness, which I don't think most people realise for an actor. It's almost having certain kinds of secrets for yourself that you'll let the whole world in on only for a moment, when you're acting. But everybody is always tugging at you. They'd all like sort of a chunk of you.

Marilyn Monroe

Acting deals with very delicate emotions. It is not putting up a mask. Each time an actor acts he does not hide; he exposes himself.

Rodney Dangerfield

My first real kiss came when I was 10, and it was in an acting class. I had to do a scene from a movie where someone gets kissed under a tree, and I did not want to do it! But my acting partner wanted me to feel comfortable, so he bought a picnic basket with all these snacks. He made such an effort - and it was cute.

Vanessa Hudgens

With any part you play, there is a certain amount of yourself in it. There has to be, otherwise it's just not acting. It's lying.

Johnny Depp

To me, teamwork is the beauty of our sport, where you have five acting as one. You become selfless.

Mike Krzyzewski

I hate people saying anything stupid. I don't really suffer fools very well at all. When people are acting like idiots, not that I'm not guilty of doing the odd idiotic thing myself from time to time, but when people say stupid things, it stresses me out.

Joshua Jackson

To start telling people that you're beautiful, or just feel beautiful, just start acting like you are the most beautiful woman in the world. And it really improves everything! Because your sort of psyche responds to it - like this is truthful!

Margaret Cho

Sarcasm is weird. Even not in acting, in life I feel like 'sarcastic' is a word that people use to describe me sometimes so when I meet someone, it's almost like they feel like they have to also be sarcastic, but it can sometimes just come off as mean if it's not used in the right way.

Aubrey Plaza

Acting is not about being someone different. It's finding the similarity in what is apparently different, then finding myself in there.

Meryl Streep

A truly good book teaches me better than to read it. I must soon lay it down, and commence living on its hint. What I began by reading, I must finish by acting.

Henry David Thoreau

Modeling is really silent acting.

Arizona Muse

With modeling, you pose. You want to look your best all the time.

With acting, you have to be aware of the camera, but the more you show your imperfections, the better you're going to be.

Diane Kruger

Hypocrisy is not a way of getting back to the moral high ground. Pretending you're moral, saying your moral is not the same as acting morally.

Alan Dershowitz

Comedy is acting out optimism.

Robin Williams

The two worst strategic mistakes to make are acting prematurely and letting an opportunity slip; to avoid this, the warrior treats each situation as if it were unique and never resorts to formulae, recipes or other people's opinions.

Paulo Coelho

Look around. Oil companies guzzle down the billions in profits. Billionaires pay a lower tax rate than their secretaries, and Wall Street CEOs, the same ones the direct our economy and destroyed millions of jobs still strut around Congress, no shame, demanding favors, and acting like we should thank them. Does anyone here have a problem with that?

Elizabeth Warren

I love acting. Acting is a true love of mine, acting and math. Although they are both creative, they use very different sides of your brain. And I love both. Acting is my first love, and that's my main career, it really is.

Danica McKellar

My goal has always been not to look forward to the next thing, but to relish and celebrate the successes I have at the moment. Whether it's landing a part in a student film or having a good day in acting class, I never discredit anything.

Dianna Agron

What I enjoy most is travelling to different places and meeting new people. For me, it's all about life experiences, and I'm very grateful that acting allows me so many interesting and fulfilling ones.

Jensen Ackles

You've got to know what you want. This is central to acting on your intentions. When you know what you want, you realize that all there is left then is time management. You'll manage your time to achieve your goals because you clearly know what you're trying to achieve in your life.

Patch Adams

Doing 'All Good Things' really felt like I was acting for myself rather than anyone else. It gave me a freedom I'd never had before, or knew I had, to do whatever I want to, and to argue my opinions and not just feel like the cute girl on set or the girl in a boy's club. I figured out how I could be both. And it's been different ever since.

Kirsten Dunst

It's easy for me to play bad guys because it's a very linear acting. Bad guys aren't empathetic. Being a bad guy is great because you're not friendly and you don't have to do much with your face.

Henry Rollins

Perhaps being old is having lighted rooms inside your head, and people in them, acting. People you know, yet can't quite name.

Francois de La Rochefoucauld

Acting provides the fulfillment of never being fulfilled. You're never as good as you'd like to be. So there's always something to hope for.

Washington Irving

A word does not frighten the man who, in acting, feels no fear.

Sophocles

Faked enthusiasm is worse than bad acting - it is bad acting with the intent to deceive.

Bo Bennett

Some scenes you juggle two balls, some scenes you juggle three balls, some scenes you can juggle five balls. The key is always to speak in your own voice. Speak the truth. That's Acting 101. Then you start putting layers on top of that.

John Burroughs

Acting helped me as I was growing up. It helped me learn about myself, helped me travel, helped me understand life, express myself, all those wonderful things. So I'm very, very grateful; it's a fun job. It's a luxury.

Angelina Jolie

Without wonder and insight, acting is just a trade. With it, it becomes creation.

Bette Davis

When people call me God, I say, no, I'm still an angel or saint of acting. I still have a long way to go.

Shahrukh Khan

What do I love about acting? I love traveling, meeting new people, exploring and just doing what I love.

Bailee Madison

I think it's a shame when you come across young actors and musicians who haven't had the time to learn their craft. It doesn't matter if it's acting or music; you really have to learn how to do it from the bottom up because unless you have a great work ethic... fame is a terrible thing to have.

Denis Leary

A large part of acting is just pretending. You get to work with these other great make-believers, all making believe as hard as they can.

Jeff Bridges

Acting is everybody's favorite second job.

Jack Nicholson

I honestly don't even know how I got into acting. It happened so quickly because my mom and sister used to do commercials, and apparently when I was little I would unbuckle myself from the stroller and crash their auditions.

Bailee Madison

My stepdad provided me with an amazing childhood. I played outside like a normal kid, I rode my bike, I walked to school, but the happiest times were when I was acting.

Demi Lovato

I had all the usual ambition growing up. I wanted to be a writer, a musician, a hockey player. I wanted to do something that wasn't nine to five. Acting was the first thing I tried that clicked.

Michael J. Fox

As a kid, I was into music, played guitar in a band. Then I started acting in plays in junior high school and just got lost in the puzzle of acting, the magic of it. I think it was an escape for me.

Michael J. Fox

The logic was, there weren't too many female comedians, so I thought I might as well try a field that had fewer competitors than the field I was in, which was acting, singing and dancing.

Rita Rudner

People think that if you look fairly reasonable, you can't possibly act, and as I only care about acting, I think beauty can be a great handicap.

Vivien Leigh

I make preparations both to live and to die every day, but with the emphasis on not dying, and on acting as if I was going to carry on living.

Christopher Hitchens

I found out I had a real love for comedy and comedy writing. The logic was, there weren't too many female comedians, so I thought I might as well try a field that had fewer competitors than the field I was in, which was acting, singing and dancing.

Rita Rudner

Don't think for a moment that I'm really like any of the characters I've played. I'm not. That's why it's called 'acting'.

Leonardo DiCaprio

I'm not sure that acting is something for a grown man to be doing.

Steve McQueen

I'm kind of bipolar in my acting choices because I just want to do a little bit of everything.

Miley Cyrus

I'm an actress. It's my passion. It's - I've always lived for acting.

Sophia Loren

I don't know what that Method is. Acting is life, to me, and should be.

Vivien Leigh

If I had to start over, I'd pursue photography - probably to the exclusion of acting.

Jessica Lange

It is easier to act yourself into a new way of feeling than to feel yourself into a new way of acting.

Harry Stack Sullivan

If this acting thing doesn't work, I'd just put in my resume for NBA.com. I'm a really huge basketball fan... I'll talk all sorts of trash.

Genesis Rodriguez

Law is downstream from culture. By the time you make a law about something, you're reacting, not acting. I'd rather shape the culture.

Rick Warren

Going back to Georgiana Drew and John Drew, and my great-grandfather Maurice Barrymore, and it was such a sort of circus of odd, interesting people that loved acting.

Drew Barrymore

I don't do method acting. If I play a farmer, I'm not gonna spend 3 weeks on a chicken farm. That's a bit too much for me.

Carice van Houten

Acting is just a way of making a living, the family is life.

Denzel Washington

For me, acting was a way of taking destructive energy and doing something productive with it, and in that way it was quite a life saver.

Nicolas Cage

The Welsh people have a talent for acting that one does not find in the English. The English lack heart.

Anthony Hopkins

Acting is always a challenge.

Robert Downey, Jr.

I don't know what acting is, but I enjoy it.

Anthony Hopkins

Acting is easier - writing is more creative. The lazy man vies with the industrious.

William Shatner

I'm not an anarchist any more. I still love the Sex Pistols, but I don't want to be a punk rocker all the time, but I do want to carry on exploring new forms of acting.

Nicolas Cage

I think when you're just counting on your voice, you actually need double the energy. I find myself acting out the scenes and being very physical while I'm recording because I think you can tell when someone is just sitting on a stool.

Judy Greer

Acting is not that far from mental disease: An actor works on splitting his character into others. It is like a kind of schizophrenia.

Vittorio Gassman

The acting thing is so beyond my control. Acting isn't mine. You're like a tiny piece in this big, corporate mechanism that needs chemistry and divine intervention.

Sandra Bullock

What I love about photography, and it's the same thing I love about acting, really, is that it forces you, like, right into the moment, where you can't be distracted, where you can't be, like, thinking about other things or ahead of yourself or behind yourself.

Jessica Lange

Actors today go into TV, which I don't consider has a lot to do with acting.

Lauren Bacall

I've not taken like acting lessons or anything but it doesn't mean I don't need to because I'm sure I do.

Miley Cyrus

I need to go where people are serious about acting.

Meryl Streep

Acting is like any other art form, in that you have the option to go very big or go very small.

Nicolas Cage

My mother was a dancer, so I like to use the body as part of the instrument of acting.

Nicolas Cage

When I was younger, I started taking singing lessons and dance and acting. I just started acting first because that's how everything happened.

Lindsay Lohan

The art of acting is not to act. Once you show them more, what you show them, in fact is bad acting.

Anthony Hopkins

I tried acting, liked it, and stuck with it. I saw it as the way I would keep that promise to myself of getting back at those who had made my school life a misery.

Anthony Hopkins

The spirit of revelation is available to every person who receives by proper priesthood authority the saving ordinances of baptism by immersion for the remission of sins and the laying on of hands for the gift of the Holy Ghost - and who is acting in faith to fulfill the priesthood injunction to 'receive the Holy Ghost.'

David A. Bednar

Because I came out as a singer, I took the time to get an acting coach.

Aaliyah

For me, acting was always a way to explore emotions - to dip into the well and really try to reach rock bottom down there. That was the most exciting part of it. I hadn't found anything that really allowed me to do that until I came upon acting.

Jessica Lange

Once I got started acting I loved it.

Jack Nicholson

I need to be performing. I need to be acting. I need to be designing a condo and ripping down walls and buying new plates and looking at fashion magazines. There always has to be some movement in the artistic department for me to not get really, really low.

Alanis Morissette

I'm involved in some action scenes, so they'll train me for that. I'll be working with my acting coach to prepare for my character.

Aaliyah

The Irish Catholic side was married to the life of an actor and I found out acting could be a form of prayer.

Liam Neeson

The wonderful thing about acting is that you can use all of your talents and interests in your work.

Jeff Bridges

Acting is just a process of relaxation, actually. Knowing the text so well and trusting that the instinct and the subconscious mind, whatever you want to call it, is going to take over.

Anthony Hopkins

I quit acting when I was 11 because I was cast as a bouncing ball in 'Alice in Wonderland,' and I felt slighted and wounded.

Lena Dunham

It is indeed hard for the strong to be just to the weak, but acting justly always has its rewards.

Eamon de Valera

Film acting is one of the only industries where you're criticized for working hard. In any other industry, it's considered a quality and something to behold.

Nicolas Cage

It is really funny to see people that you know acting unpleasantly just because there are TV cameras on.

Penn Jillette

People acting in their own self-interest is the fuel for all the discovery, innovation, and prosperity that powers the world.

John Stossel

My approach to acting is that I am totally intuitive. I read the script and I get it. If I don't get it, I can't do it.

Morgan Freeman

It was only when I realized how actors have the power to move people that I decided to pursue acting as a career.

Cate Blanchett

Acting is a form of confusion.

Tallulah Bankhead

Dane DeHaan, certainly, is kind of the best friend I've made through acting, in terms of another actor. He's fantastic.

Daniel Radcliffe

Just let the wardrobe do the acting.

Jack Nicholson

Acting still rings my bell as much as it did in high school. Plus, I can now indulge my interests as a producer as well. My work is more fun than fun but, best of all, it's still very scary. You are always walking some kind of high wire.

Tom Hanks

If I spent all my time criticising myself, I wouldn't be able to function. There are actors who theorise till the cows come home. I haven't the patience for them. It's maybe shallow, but that's why I'll never be part of the acting set.

Anthony Hopkins

I like acting for now. But after seeing Apollo 13, what I really want to do is to be an astronaut. I'm dying to go to a space camp next summer!

Natalie Portman

As a rapper, you sort of act in music videos and in the persona you adopt onstage. You kinda have to put yourself out there and be courageous even to be a rapper. So, to step into acting was not that difficult a transition to make.

Queen Latifah

Before acting, I wanted to become a journalist. I also toyed with the idea of being a chef - but that's only when people asked me what I wanted to be. In fact, I always used to say I wanted to be an actor, but I didn't ever believe that I was good enough to be come one.

Ian Mckellen

One good thing about acting in film is that it's good therapy.

Denzel Washington

Having been an actor and a writer for so long - 20 years or so - I felt that it would be daft to go to one's grave without having directed. It's a natural extension of writing and acting, and so I knew it would happen one day.

Stephen Fry

I find that kid actors are great reminders of the simplicity of acting. As you get older, you can sometimes complicate things a little more. You can become too aware of, 'Okay, this is the scene emotionally. This is where we need to be. We've got the climax coming up.' You can start to analyze it too much.

Hugh Jackman

Acting is the hardest job in the entire world. By far. Harder than ditch digging.

Paul Thomas Anderson

Partying and having all of those pictures taken distracts from the work that I do. It's not why I started acting. I didn't get into acting to be written about. It kind of just happened - so I accept that it's my life.

Lindsay Lohan

It's got to do with putting yourself in other people's shoes and seeing how far you can come to truly understand them. I like the empathy that comes from acting.

Christian Bale

I know some really great actors who are pretty judgmental people, pretty critical people. But they're great actors. When they're acting, that's the craft.

Philip Seymour Hoffman

I've got to see my movie to see how I'm acting, see what little things I can learn about my craft.

LL Cool J

My parents never looked at my acting as a career. They saw it as a way to help provide for the household.

Paul Walker

Acting is a sense of wonder and magic and mystery for me and when life takes me on a new journey, I simply remember the smile my first ballet recital put on my face and I move forward.

Andrea Thompson

Acting is a masochistic form of exhibitionism. It is not quite the occupation of an adult.

Laurence Olivier

Directing is much more satisfying to me than acting.

George Clooney

I mean, there's chemistry in life and there's acting chemistry. I'm not saying they're the same thing, but they're as mysterious.

David Duchovny

Acting is the only thing I'm even vaguely good at and acting is something that I think I do know about.

Martin Freeman

I like talking. I like acting.

Denzel Washington

I prefer the smaller acting than big histrionics. It's about reacting and looks, which is often underestimated.

Viggo Mortensen

A lot of people in my world - in the acting world - have either lost friends to Aids or live with HIV because its origin in our culture, in New York for instance, was in the gay community.

Emma Thompson

My professional acting life, stage and screen, has brought me public support, emotional fulfillment and material comfort. It has brought me together with fine people, good companions with whom I've shared the inevitable lot of all actors: flops and hits.

Peter O'Toole

I like singing as much as I like acting, and all through high school I thought I might be a Broadway singer.

Zooey Deschanel

When I was at school, I was terrible at algebra and arithmetic, but I was always the best at English and literature. And acting, of course.

Joan Collins

Acting allows me to explore new worlds, to discover characters by delving into their lives, and ultimately to become someone else entirely.

Pierce Brosnan

You can't have bank holding companies acting as hedge funds. You can't have them taking a million-dollar pension plan for Joe Schmo the bus driver and treat it with the same risk appetite that you treat George Soros' pocket money. It's fundamentally ridiculous.

Shia LaBeouf

Well, acting itself is a form of rebellion, always. Getting up there in front of people, telling stories - you're kind of going against the grain to begin with, wanting to do that, don't you think? Why else would you do it? Except maybe as kind of a way to affirm your very existence.

John Cusack

Improv as an actor makes you present in the moment. You listen, you're attentive. You're not acting so much as reacting, which is what you're doing in life all the time.

Nathan Fillion

Stardom is only a by-product of acting. I don't think being a movie star is a good enough reason for existing.

Natalie Wood

Acting is the most brotherly and sisterly profession in the world.

Cyril Cusack

Sometimes a scene works and acting is the easiest thing in the world and you don't have to do much of anything - just enjoy yourself and listen to the other actor. When it doesn't work, then every actor has different ways of dealing with the impasse. Sometimes you use memories from the past. Whatever. It depends from job to job.

Viggo Mortensen

If you want to surf, move to Hawaii. If you like to shop, move to New York. If you like acting and Hollywood, move to California. But if you like college football, move to Texas.

Ricky Williams

I've personally never wanted to be 'the babe', and refuse to let vanity get in the way of my acting because I don't see my job as being a beautiful person.

Zooey Deschanel

I'm surrounded by friends and family who are not that impressed by celebrity. They don't have any problem telling me I'm acting like an idiot or I'm not that funny.

Paloma Faith

I have quite a rich inner life, and I'm constantly looking for a way to express that. I haven't found it yet in acting. When you're playing a character, you're only going to find outlets for very specific parts of your inner world.

Daniel Radcliffe

One of the things I like about acting is that, in a funny way, I come back to myself.

Bill Murray

I think the point to be understood is that we're all different. I've never been a fan of theories of acting. I didn't go to drama school, so I was never put through a training that was limited by someone saying, 'This is the way you should act.'

Ian Mckellen

Acting is all about big hair and funny props... All the great actors knew it. Olivier knew it, Brando knew it.

Harold Ramis

I have driven school buses, sold egg rolls and painted houses, and I have often wondered what my life would have been like if I hadn't gone into acting. Mind you, it's a great life, going around pretending you're other people and getting paid ridiculous sums of money for it.

John Malkovich

It never occurred to me that I was a leading man until I was 19 years old. I had been acting since I was 10, so that's nine years and 30 or 40 plays, in school and summer stock, professional theater, too.

Christopher Reeve

You can see all sorts of things in film acting if you know where to look and what to look for. One thing I often notice is that the actor is looking for his mark, the place where he has to stand to be in the right place in the shot.

Michael Caine

I've been planted here to be a vessel for acting... That's why I'm really taking any part, regardless of how complicated it's going to be.

Leonardo DiCaprio

I remember being a little kid sitting in the living room with my brother and some friends from around the neighborhood, and I would sit at the piano and as they were running around the room doing different things and being silly, acting out, I would actually play the score for it - the music that went along with it.

Mike Shinoda

For me, acting is doing.

Pierce Brosnan

If you want to be a screenwriter, take an acting class to get a sense of what you're asking actors to do. Learning other skills will help you communicate with people and respect what they do.

Tina Fey

All I have to say is basically if performing, singing, acting ,and dancing is what you want to do, then you just have to do it - no matter where it is.

Ariana Grande

I was the youngest child and really spoiled. I loved to play make-believe. I loved pretending to be all kinds of different people and it just seemed natural that I would go into acting.

Katherine Heigl

I love the acting community at Cambridge. It's really quite committed and serious, since the days of Derek Jacobi and Ian McKellen right through to Emma Thompson and Hugh Laurie.

Tom Hiddleston

Singing is a way of releasing an emotion that you sometimes can't portray when you're acting. And music moves your soul, so music is the source of the most intense emotions you can feel.

Amanda Seyfried

Acting is largely about putting on masks, and music is about removing them.

Hugh Laurie

Acting is invigorating. But I don't analyse it too much. It's like a dog smelling where it's going to do its toilet in the morning.

Liam Neeson

I love acting because it's a bit of an escape. It gives you the ability to reinvent yourself. They say that acting is the shy man's revenge.

Hayden Christensen

I wanted to go to acting school, and I did a few modeling jobs to pay for acting school. I never aspired to be a model. I met lots of photographers, and I learned a lot about light - as a source of love and illumination, light as a gift of love. On film, that's a massive contribution.

Jacqueline Bisset

I just let the work speak for itself. An actor is not afraid to take risks; to put on different hats; to be a good guy, a bad guy, a victim, an abuser. There are all kinds of people in the world, and playing them is what acting is all about.

Kevin Bacon

I mean, sometimes... a comedian becomes an actor, and they just don't deliver, because the bottom line of comedy is to be funny, and the bottom line of acting is to be truthful, and they get that mixed up sometimes, or don't even notice that that's the thing.

Eddie Izzard

Acting is such a personal thing, which is weird because at the same time it's not. It's for the consumption of other people. But in terms of creative outlets and expressing yourself, it's just the most extreme version of that that I've ever found. It's like running, it's exertion.

Kristen Stewart

You have to come in and be that character when you walk into the room. That's what one of my first acting teachers taught me. You know, don't go in there being Jennifer and then expect to flip and change, because they're not going to have that imagination.

Jennifer Lopez

I was studying to be an architect, I wasn't plotting to join the movies. Films were just another career option. I took acting up with the same schoolgirl enthusiasm I had for examinations. Acting is a job and I take it very seriously.

Aishwarya Rai Bachchan

Acting has to do with saying it as if you meant it, so for me the words are always very important. It's very important for me to know my lines, know them so well that I don't have to think about them.

Christopher Walken

You bring out a lot of your own thoughts and attitudes when acting. I think a great deal of it has to do with the inner you.

Ginger Rogers

I find what I do for a living really funny. I mean, acting is kind of a hilarious thing for a grown man to call a job.

Christian Bale

Macbeth is a very popular play with audiences. If you want to sell out a theater, just mount a production of Macbeth. It's a short play, it's an exciting play, it's easy to understand, and it attracts great acting.

Ian Mckellen

I'm sure acting is a deeply neurotic thing to do.

Ralph Fiennes

My family was going back to England to visit my mother's grandmother, who was very ill. We went up to Liverpool and I met my great-aunt, who was just a force of nature. She was an elocution teacher and a huge enthusiast for theater and the classics. I took her amateur acting class, and she was really impressed with me.

Kim Cattrall

Acting is the most wildly overpaid position imaginable.

Robert Downey, Jr.

I went from being totally unknown and never acting professionally to being in a major movie and being very famous. It all happened so quickly, I didn't have any time to work things out. It's been pretty scary at times.

Emma Watson

Acting is like lying. The art of lying well. I'm paid to tell elaborate lies.

Mel Gibson

I start from scratch with each movie; I wipe the slate and I certainly don't rely on some bag of acting tricks I've amassed over the years.

Christian Bale

Acting is the work of two people - it's only possible when you have the complicity, the help, even the manipulation of a director.

Victoria Abril

Acting is a bit like being an athlete. You spend all your time getting ready to do something for two minutes. All the things that made my career in the movies happen took two or three minutes, which is the time that it takes for a 'take'. In that time, something happens. That's what people know you for, just like someone running the hundred metres.

Christopher Walken

Once I start putting all my little insecurities in my mind, I'm not actually acting. Then it's about me - and it should never be about me. It should be about the character.

Nicole Kidman

In acting, I always try to go back to what would actually be the real situation, the real human behavior in life.

Robert De Niro

I'm very aware that when one is acting in the theater, you do become kind of animal about it. And you're reliant on instincts rather than tact a lot of the time.

Alan Rickman

Well, I think one of the main things that you have to think about when acting in the movies is to try not to make the acting show.

James Stewart

When I left school, I got a job in a shoe shop and I used to save 15 quid a week and pay for my own singing and acting lessons.

Luke Evans

It shouldn't come as any surprise that those who choose acting as a profession are phonies who live in a fantasy world. What is surprising is how many of them are blissfully unaware of it.

Julie Burchill

I remember hearing someone say that good acting is more about taking off a mask than putting one on, and in movie acting, certainly that's true. With the camera so close, you can see right down into your soul, hopefully. So being able to do that in a way is terrifying, and in another way, truly liberating. And I like that about it.

Annette Bening

I have actual acting scars.

Benedict Cumberbatch

Someone will always hate what I say. There's always going to be somebody spitting blood about my wooden-faced, toffee-named, crappy acting.

Benedict Cumberbatch

For me, acting comes straight from the heart. In that sense I don't act at all. I think that to feel the character's pain I have to be myself. Somewhere audiences see that.

Salman Khan

'Johnny' was always a lone wolf when he got on stage. Him against the world, whereas suddenly, when I got into acting, people were relying on me.

Johnny Vegas

So much of movie acting is in the lighting. And in loving your characters. I try to know them, and with that intimacy comes love. And now, I love Voldemort.

Ralph Fiennes

I don't know about living on an automatic pilot, but I've had times where I've decided to just test myself and my mettle, and for no good reason other than it's what life is. Even before I was acting, I had, like, one day in high school I decided to just show them my pajamas, just for no good reason.

Will Ferrell

Look up the definition of rejection in the dictionary, get really comfortable with it, and then maybe you can go into acting.

Loni Anderson

Acting is a humiliating job, from start to finish.

Claire Danes

It's important to have people around you with enough confidence to say if you are not acting in a good way. Normally, when you are at the top, people say everything is fantastic. Probably in that moment it is what you want to hear, but it's best to be reminded how to act properly.

Rafael Nadal

I don't want to discredit people's individuality, but I think people are pretty much the same. People are very similar. If you have a good enough imagination then you can feel things that you personally have never done before. That's acting.

Kristen Stewart

I started acting pretty young, so I haven't had too many odd jobs. But I used to sell candy out of my locker in middle school.

Paul Dano

There is a growing frustration that the EU is seen as something that is done to people rather than acting on their behalf. And this is being intensified by the very solutions required to resolve the economic problems.

David Cameron

Doing acting opened up other creative outlets; it made me feel freer as an artist.

Common

If you followed this economic crisis and you do not think that the world is getting flatter, you are not paying attention. We saw the entire global economy at one time acting totally in sync. The real truth is the world is even flatter than I thought. Our mortgage crisis is killing Deutsche Bank. You still don't think the world is flat?

Thomas Friedman

The art of acting is to be other than what you are.

Whoopi Goldberg

Bad acting is the ultimate inconsideration.

Debra Winger

I went through this realization that acting, at its heart, is the ability to manipulate your own emotions.

Scarlett Johansson

Acting is something different to everybody. I just know that if you watch an actor or actress getting better and better, I think that's them just understanding themselves better and better.

Cameron Diaz

All the theories that acting is reacting to imaginary circumstances as though they are real, and directing is turning psychology into behavior, those are all stabs at something that can't be taught. All the great actors can't talk about what they do, and they don't want to begin to talk about it. They just do it.

Mike Nichols

I don't let it bother me too much if someone doesn't like me. I just figure there's no accounting for taste. It's not me, it's my acting. It's like if someone doesn't like someone's food, they just don't like my acting.

Anna Chlumsky

I loved plays, I loved films, but I had no desire to act until I had just put out my album 'Like Water for Chocolate.' Creatively, I felt like I'd hit a ceiling, and I needed something else to express myself, and I just decided to take acting classes.

Common

A man who waits to believe in action before acting is anything you like, but he's not a man of action. You must act as you breathe.

Georges Clemenceau

I owe my whole acting career to the fact that I'm a singer. I went out to Los Angeles and auditioned for a TV show called 'Fame L.A.' The original role was for a comedian, but they said I wasn't very funny, so they asked me, 'What else can you do?' So I played a singer.

Christian Kane

I've always remembered something Sanford Meisner, my acting teacher, told us. When you create a character, it's like making a chair, except instead of making someting out of wood, you make it out of yourself. That's the actor's craft - using yourself to create a character.

Robert Duvall

I'm a good acting partner for me... when I don't have anyone else, I do really well!

Elaine Stritch

I had just arrived in New York from California. I was nineteen years old and excited beyond belief. I was an art student and an acting student and behaved as most young actors did - meaning that there was no such thing as a good actor, 'cause you yourself hadn't shown up yet.

Robert Redford

I knew that I wanted to be an actor; how to go about it was the question. I went to Australia for my studies; from there I told my dad that I also want to do a course in performing arts, but my father refused. So I completed my studies and came back. But I kept poking him, saying that acting is something that I want to do.

Randeep Hooda

I love the art of acting, so I don't care if I'm in a movie with 10 people, two people, or by myself. I just really enjoy it.

Taraji P. Henson

I never lost my interest in acting but I did lose my interest in the business and what I had to go through to make a film. I felt saturated, you know, like a sponge when it's saturated - it's not good.

Debra Winger

Acting just happens to be my skill, but I think I would probably be just as happy being a technician or entering into the film business in some other way.

Jodie Foster

For me acting is a passion and an art, and always will only be that. I don't have any rules when it comes to acting. I'll do anything. But it depends on the script. Either I'll have passion for the project or I won't. It's got to fuel me.

Shailene Woodley

When everyone around you is doing all this incredible pirate acting and you're having to sort of play the straight guy and move the story forward, you kind of want to be doing some of that pirate ripping it up stuff, but in truth, to be a part of that project is what I love.

Orlando Bloom

The enemy resembles us. Therefore, he needs to be approached not as an assembly of 'targets' to be destroyed one by one; but as a living, intelligent entity capable of acting and reacting.

Martin Van Creveld

Once I accomplish one thing and I'm satisfied, I try something else. I may be 50 and doing something totally outside of music and acting. Maybe I'll become a kindergarten teacher.

Kid Cudi

God is acting on your soul all the time, whether you have spiritual sensations or not.

Evelyn Underhill

I never took an acting class, so I've made all my mistakes on film.

Heath Ledger

When I came out to L. A., I got a part in an episode of 'Star Trek: Voyager,' and I hired an acting coach.

Sarah Silverman

I write all the time because I'm lonely. When you're acting, you're working every day all day. But then you have long amounts of time off.

Jesse Eisenberg

I think of myself as an entertainment arsenal. Like I have my acting bazooka and my music machete. And you don't know what I'm going to come at you with.

Jack Black

I got so far away from what they told you in acting class: Do something different. Producers kept offering me the 'Sister Act' movie, but I said, 'My fans don't want to see me in a wimple.' I literally said, 'My fans don't want to see me in a wimple.'

Bette Midler

Christ does not save us by acting a parable of divine love; he acts the parable of divine love by saving us. That is the Christian faith.

Austin Farrer

It's all about hustling, whether it's in Boston or the film industry. I've been hustling my entire life - acting my way into trouble and acting my way back out again. I'm just fortunate to have had the opportunity to apply it in a different direction.

Mark Wahlberg

For me, acting goes to a special place; it's almost mystical. You have to let go of what you think is good; it's a jump into trust, and trying to reach without wanting too much.

Juliette Binoche

I don't know when acting came to be more about awards than about the work. Judging who's better than the other person shouldn't be part of why we're doing this job. It should be about entertaining people.

Anna Paquin

I think theatre is by far the most rewarding experience for an actor. You get 4 weeks to rehearse your character and then at 7:30 pm you start acting and nobody stops you, acting with your entire soul.

Christopher Eccleston

I was very interested in theatre, mostly in stage design. I did a little bit of acting.

Jim Henson

The most significant piece of advice my father gave me early on about acting was, don't get caught acting. Really believe in what you're doing and then commit to it. Even if it feels uncomfortable, even if you feel that you're gonna look like an ass. It's all acting, but find the truth in a moment as opposed to just pretending you have and rather than trying to act your way out of it.

Kiefer Sutherland

Acting is such a huge part of my life. It really allows me to have a creative outlet and to actually be able to have an outlet to discuss openly the things that truly I think are relevant in the world, that make a difference.

Ian Somerhalder

I don't hate myself anymore. I used to hate my work, hated that sexy image, hated those pictures of me onstage, hated that big raunchy person. Onstage, I'm acting the whole time I'm there. As soon as I get out of those songs, I'm Tina again.

Tina Turner

In L.A., I was meeting people who were all actors. My mind started to open up to what acting was. I didn't realize that Brad Pitt was a real person. I didn't think he was a robot or a machine, but I thought you were just born into acting - that it's a family tree, kind of like NASCAR. No one can just say, 'Hey, I'm going to be a NASCAR driver.'

Kellan Lutz

It's always at the back of my mind that acting might come to an end for me when Harry Potter finishes. I don't know if I'm good enough to have a long career. I've got a bit of an inferiority complex about my acting. My self-esteem is quite low in that sense.

Rupert Grint

I don't think acting is addictive. If I stopped acting tomorrow, I really wouldn't care. If you told me that I would have to sell real estate in New York City to look after my family, that would be fine with me.

Alec Baldwin

There's sketch, improv, writing, acting, music, and badminton. Those are the seven forms of comedy.

T. J. Miller

I like going in to different styles of acting and exploring stuff I haven't done before.

Mel Gibson

When I got to college, acting suddenly seemed like a very risky proposition and all my friends were going to law school or med school or Wall Street.

Wentworth Miller

It's a trap I've fallen into earlier in my career - trying to be liked. Don't do it. When I watch TV and I see someone trying to make me like them, acting cute or quirky or goofy, I'm not impressed. Don't act like America's watching you. Just latch onto your character. Characters are flawed. Be unlikeable. Be flawed. Be a person.

Nathan Fillion

White people are very good at acting like they're not racist. They deserve an Academy Award for that.

Paul Mooney

Acting is all about truth and honesty, and the sensitivity that's capable of transporting you.

Thomas Kretschmann

At least when you're acting you can be someone. In front of the camera you have to be yourself. And who am I?

Stephen Rea

I always loved acting and improv and sketch comedy and theater, which I did at a local youth theater.

Emma Stone

To be an icon is a big job - it's beyond acting. And sometimes it pays, and sometimes it doesn't.

Isabella Rossellini

Acting itself is quite scary. Some people say that actors are show-offs, very egotistical and all that kind of stuff, but it is quite scary.

Michael Sheen

I'm disappointed in acting as a craft. I want everything to go back to Orson Welles and fake noses and changing your voice. It's become so much about personality.

Spencer Tracy

I have the opportunity to learn about the fashion world, and I appreciate it as an art form... But I never want it to take over my acting.

Lupita Nyong'o

You don't see Indians in Hollywood films around which a story can revolve. As soon as we have a social presence in your society, I am sure there will be many actors from our part of the world that will be acting in Hollywood films.

Amitabh Bachchan

I got the acting bug back because I felt like all of a sudden maybe after all these years, maybe I might have something to offer again. I walked away from it after 'Signs' because I just felt I was a bit stale and it wasn't ringing my bells, so I focused on directing, writing and producing.

Mel Gibson

For me, I guess I'm the acting equivalent of somebody that jumps off buildings and parachutes.

Joaquin Phoenix

Acting is standing up naked and turning around very slowly.

Rosalind Russell

I love acting, truly my favorite people are actors.

Sean Penn

I just thought acting would be something to help out with my student loans, but my first year as an actress, I made more money than my parents. That's when I realized it could turn into a career. After that, I put everything I had into it.

Gabrielle Union

I believe that being an actress or being involved in a movie has to be a life experience, otherwise why go for it? I have to change me, and I have to learn things, and I have to push me and my limits. By acting, I find a freedom inside of a prison in a way.

Juliette Binoche

I didn't go to acting school, but I've been observing my fellow man for 66 years now, and I would think that's the best school there is.

Wilford Brimley

A huge part of acting in movies is appetite. You do your best work when you've got a lot of appetite and you really want to embrace something. When you get tired, you don't have that hunger.

Clive Owen

A lot of the time I hate acting. It has a lot to do with the way I was brought up in a world where showing your emotions is frowned upon. It's just not manly. I don't do anything in life because I love doing it. It's because I want to be good at it.

Matthew Fox

Acting is a matter of giving away secrets.

Ellen Barkin

I just enjoy acting, whatever area - theatre, film, television.

Michelle Dockery

Whether it's repro rights, violence against women, or just plain old vanilla sexism, most issues affecting women have one thing in common - they exist to keep women 'in their place.' To make sure that we're acting 'appropriately,' whatever that means.

Jessica Valenti

I've never lost my appetite for acting; it's innovative and challenging.

Eli Wallach

I like acting for myself as a director. I act and I know that I'll have a chance to have some say in what gets used and that I'll be able to give myself enough takes and be on the same page as myself about how the scene should play.

Ben Affleck

I don't have a great talent for explaining myself in acting because I can't explain it.

Elaine Stritch

I must say acting was good training for the political life which lay ahead for us.

Nancy Reagan

It's so funny, you go to acting school thinking you're going to learn how to be other people, but really it taught me how to be myself. Because it's in understanding yourself deeply that you can lend yourself to another person's circumstances and another person's experience.

Lupita Nyong'o

In Chicago it's really a case of the play's the thing - people are just so happy to be acting, you know? We were all actors - not like in New York or Los Angeles, where everyone says they are actors but they are actually waiting tables and hustling for spots in commercials.

John C. Reilly

There are kids who get on a BMX bike when they're eight years old and they go, 'Whoa, this is incredible,' and grow up to do extreme sports. It's the same for me with acting.

Joaquin Phoenix

I feel when acting, I am sometimes overly self-conscious; I think, 'Going, no, don't, put your eyebrow back where it was and, you know, turn to the left.' You know, I'm sort of very consciously adopting this character. But with music, I don't know. I found it was a question of just closing my eyes and just sort of letting things come out.

Hugh Laurie

But acting is very much a profession that is you're hot one moment and not the next - and that is totally cool. I think that's what I find most fascinating and most exciting about it - is that it can be gone in a puff of smoke.

Keira Knightley

Singing was my first love and I never even considered it after I started acting, but now I'm bringing it back into my life. I trained from the ages of 11 to 17. When I moved to New York and got into serious acting, I just kind of abandoned the whole singing thing. But when I grew up in Pennsylvania I went to voice lessons once a week.

Amanda Seyfried

If I am able to carry on modeling, I'll be very happy to, but my passion is definitely in music and acting. I would love to do what Meryl Streep is doing. Her or Judi Dench, or maybe Charlize Theron as well.

Cara Delevingne

I really think that effective acting has to do literally with the movement of molecules.

Charlotte Whitton

I think to be courageous, you have to be afraid. For me, it feels very courageous when I go skiing because I'm very, very afraid to ski. It's dangerous! I feel very scared. But when I'm acting, I don't feel very scared.

Julianne Moore

I was always very creative. I was always into acting and dancing when I was younger.

Marina and the Diamonds

My acting range has always been something between the two extremes of 'raises left eyebrow' and 'raises right eyebrow.'

Roger Moore

I wanted to be involved in TV and film in some capacity, so a compromise, because acting seemed unrealistic, and so risky, was to get into the production side. And it was a really fortunate, smart move looking back on it, because it gave me perspective on another side of the business.

Wentworth Miller

I want to be uncomfortable - acting is uncomfortable.

Lupita Nyong'o

I did a film called 'Floating' early on that had a scene which was similar to a real-life situation I was in at the time. It involved me having a conversation with my father, who was dying. It was close to home and it made me realise acting wasn't just making faces for the cameras, it was a real art form.

Norman Reedus

You have to believe what you say, and if you believe what you are saying, then acting is easy.

Jean-Claude Van Damme

Pretending to be other people is my game and that to me is the essence of the whole business of acting.

John Hurt

It's not just that individuals have lost faith in the integrity of their leaders, it's that they no longer believe society's most powerful institutions are acting in their interests.

Gary Hamel

Never get caught acting.

Lillian Gish

My mother worked for a woman, Maria Ley-Piscator, who with her husband founded the Dramatic Workshop, which was connected to the New School. My mother did proofreading and typing and stuff or her, and as part of her payment, I was able to take acting classes there on Saturdays when I was 10.

Robert De Niro

When you're young, working in a warehouse or selling hot dogs, you look at work - at acting - as something precious. It gets you out of the stink.

Mickey Rourke

A friend of my mom's was a casting director so, really as kind of a lark, I had a couple of acting jobs that had just enough exposure to give me the option to continue if I wanted to. I followed through with it.

Ben Affleck

Acting is like roller skating. Once you know how to do it, it is neither stimulating nor exciting.

George Sanders

When you are acting, you are just one piece of the puzzle. You don't see how everything fits together. It feels like you have less authorship over the entire product. In directing, you take the entire picture into account, so you're challenged in a different way.

Misha Collins

The only people who have doubts about the sincerity of my music are people who come to it relatively late, off the back of having seen me in a film. Acting is about being other people, and music is about being myself.

Riz Ahmed

Leadership is the other side of the coin of loneliness, and he who is a leader must always act alone. And acting alone, accept everything alone.

Ferdinand Marcos

Leadership is a way of thinking, a way of acting and, most importantly, a way of communicating.

Simon Sinek

I can see clearly now... that I was wrong in not acting more decisively and more forthrightly in dealing with Watergate.

Richard M. Nixon

Being a former dancer, classical dancer, it informed me as a human being just in terms of the grace I guess. Ballet is a very graceful form of art. You also become very aware of your body and your mind and your body is working in conjunction. That kind of helps you in acting as well. It's not only using your mind, it's like making your mind communicate this character into your body so that you can bring it to life and physicalize it.

Zoe Saldana

When strangers start acting like neighbors... communities are reinvigorated.

Ralph Nader

I've always thought of acting as more of an exercise in empathy, which is not to be confused with sympathy. You're trying to get inside a certain emotional reality or motivational reality and try to figure out what that's about so you can represent it.

Edward Norton

Even as far back as when I started acting at 14, I know I've never considered failure.

Jennifer Lawrence

My own dreams fortunately came true in this great state. I became Mr. Universe; I became a successful businessman. And even though some people say I still speak with a slight accent, I have reached the top of the acting profession.

Arnold Schwarzenegger

Certain people are like 'Oh, here come the Feminazis!' You end up acting 10 times nicer than you even need to be, to be the opposite of the stereotype like 'You're the man haters!' We're always bending over backwards being extra nice. And I don't know if being nice is my legacy.

Kathleen Hanna

I know that if I'd had to go and take an exam for acting, I wouldn't have got anywhere. You don't take exams for acting, you take your courage.

Edith Evans

It's easy to play a bad girl: You just do everything you've been told not to do, and you don't have to deal with the consequences, because it's only acting.

Eliza Dushku

Frustration is a sign I am acting independently. The more you try your own way, the tighter the doors will stay closed.

Joyce Meyer

Life's like a play: it's not the length, but the excellence of the acting that matters.

Lucius Annaeus Seneca

The creation of something new is not accomplished by the intellect but by the play instinct acting from inner necessity. The creative mind plays with the objects it loves.

Carl Jung

My parents' divorce left me with a lot of sadness and pain and acting, and especially humour, was my way of dealing with all that.

Jennifer Aniston

Having the right people around you all the time is important. I do take the acting seriously. But this is all fun. I look at it like smoke and mirrors. I still think it's a dream, but I ain't pinching myself yet.

Chris Brown

I'm no good at anything but comedy, which I think I'm good at. I'm absolutely no good at networking; I'm terrible at acting; I'm terrible at dealing with executives; I'm terrible at collaborating. And I say whatever I want to say. But I think I'm good enough at comedy that I can survive. And I don't really have an ambition for money.

Norm MacDonald

Opponents of capital punishment argue that the state has no right to take a murderer's life. Apparently, one fact that abolitionists forget or overlook is that the state is acting not only on behalf of society, but also on behalf of the murdered person and the murdered person's family.

Dennis Prager

I'm curious about other people. That's the essence of my acting. I'm interested in what it would be like to be you.

Meryl Streep

You can take lessons to become almost anything: flying lessons, piano lessons, skydiving lessons, acting lessons, race car driving lessons, singing lessons. But there's no class for comedy. You have to be born with it. God has to give you this gift.

Steve Harvey

I think singing and acting go hand in hand. Take an R&B singer: one song says, 'I love you,' the next is, 'Baby, don't leave me', the next is, 'If you leave me I don't care.' You have to drop in and out of different perspectives.

Ice T

I could describe my career in two words: who knew. I was on the path to becoming a professional baseball player, but I got injured in college. When I decided to move out to L.A. to try acting, nobody was betting on me, not even my family. But it's always been that way for me; nothing has come easy.

Shemar Moore

Jazz music and, more specifically, jazz musicians, are my artistic heroes. I want to be the Thelonious Monk of acting. He had no concern for how well he was received. He played whatever he wanted whenever he wanted. He just wasn't interested in achieving the good opinion of his audience. That's the Holy Grail of acting; of any art form.

Trevor St. John

I can act. I've been acting for a long time, but like anything else, don't nobody owe you nothing. You've go to pay your dues. You go from A to Z; you don't go from M to Z.

Bernie Mac

We grew up in abject poverty. Acting, writing scripts and skits were a way of escaping our environment at a very young age.

Viola Davis

Acting, the arts in general, is a magnet for the wounded of society.

Robert Carlyle

Everyone has a different path. I knew no one in the acting industry growing up. I never did a play until college. I was not outspoken when I was younger and I hated being the center of attention. But I had a dream of being an actor. I went to NYU and studied theatre. I learned a craft. And began my career straight out of college.

Peter Facinelli

Most people want to become movie stars and I just want to be in the business. I already was a star. If I get the part of a lifetime and it blows up, then that's wonderful. But if the acting doesn't work, fine. I'll just be a producer. And if the producing doesn't work, fine. I've got a lot of other stuff.

Carl Lewis

What you're doing is acting with yourself. Well, I'm my favourite actor, so in a way it's quite straightforward for me.

Peter Capaldi

Acting feels different. I'm not sure exactly what that is, but it used to mean a lot more. Maybe that sounds like I'm throwing it away and

I'm not, I'll still do the best damn job I can, but it doesn't mean the same thing. I'm going to get the answer for myself one of these days. It's the male menopause, that's what it is.

Mel Gibson

When I do stand-up for a long time, I'll get burned out, then I'll get an acting gig. For me, the grass is always greener. I'd like to do a mixture of all of it. My goal is just to do small movies that I've written. That's what I'm trying to do now, just write smaller movies.

Zach Galifianakis

I acted all the way up until Princeton. It was just one of my favorite extracurricular activities. Then I got to Princeton and had a really conservative vibe. All my friends were planning on law school, med school, or Wall Street, and suddenly acting seem like a really risky proposition.

Wentworth Miller

Love is as strict as acting. If you want to love somebody, stand there and do it. If you don't, don't. There are no other choices.

Tyne Daly

I'm a natural blonde. But when I started acting, I would go to auditions and they didn't know where to put me because I was voluptuous and had the accent, but I had blonde hair. It was

67

ignorance: they thought every Latin person looks like Salma Hayek.

Sofia Vergara

Comedy's my first love. I love that so much. You play comedy in drama, too. The difference between genres doesn't really change the method of acting.

Emma Stone

Acting is a very limited form of expression and those who take it seriously are very limited people. I take it seriously.

Judy Holliday

I was an English major at UCLA when I was 18, and then I left after a year to start acting. I was educating myself during that time.

James Franco

When it comes to social consequences, they've got all different people acting in different ways, very difficult to even have a proper criterion of success. So, it's a difficult task.

George Soros

I ain't acting when I'm on stage. That's why all the little love bugs who'll come and see me at Lovebox love me. They know it's the real me.

Lil' Kim

Anything that opens you up emotionally is going to impact your acting. Parenthood, becoming a mom, certainly does that.

Keri Russell

My style is an extension of acting and an outcome of some serious lessons I picked up learning when I did theatre in my early days.

Kapil Sharma

I love to work. I really enjoy getting up really early and driving downtown. I just really love the process of acting and being on a series.

Portia de Rossi

I try to not think too much about how stuff gets seen as it's being done by a woman. Because if you think about it, then you end up thinking about how you're acting, and if you are thinking about how you're acting, then you are preoccupied and you're going to end up being insincere. You're kind of not present.

Christine Quinn

I get my exercise acting as a pallbearer to my friends who exercise.

Chauncey Depew

Movie magic is movie magic and acting magic is acting magic.

Ben Kingsley

I had fun doing it, but acting ain't really my thing. I am more of a production/director type. I would rather be behind the scenes and organizing and putting things together like that.

Dr. Dre

I was on the improv team in high school, and after I graduated, I joined an improv company that had been established 10 years prior to me getting there. They did longform improv, and I fell in love with it. It's acting, character creation, collaborative, artistic expression and comedy - and it's scary. It was a big rush.

Tatiana Maslany

I like and I love everything that has to do with cinema: writing, directing, editing, creating music, and even acting.

Werner Herzog

Music is a hobby, because I'm not making any money out of it, but I put just as much conviction into that as I do into my acting.

River Phoenix

The kind of acting I used to enjoy no longer exists because your prime consideration is the budget, running time, the cost - and whether they'll understand it in Milwaukee.

Dirk Bogarde

I like fashion, but I love, love, love music and film; they are my two passions. I would love to pursue my acting and my love of music more than anything.

Cara Delevingne

Many Republicans have always reminded me of professional W.W.F. wrestlers. They come into the ring all pumped up and acting like they're invincible and that they're going to destroy their opponent. Then they get hit once and fall down and roll around in agony and suddenly seem immobilized by pain, calling for the ref to intervene.

Paul Feig

Acting is a plum gig, and then animation is an even more plum gig.

Aziz Ansari

I was sitting in the looping studio late one night, and I had this epiphany that they weren't paying me for my acting, for God's sake, but to own me. And from then on, it became clear and an awful lot easier to deal with.

Angela Carter

Being able to do lead roles in pictures or onstage or whatever it is that you're doing in acting is obviously what you strive for because you want to better yourself as an actor and you want to better yourself as a person as well. But that does come with a lot of responsibility and a great deal of weight.

Jamie Campbell Bower

I loved acting, I started as a child and it is interesting because I didn't compare myself to others that were doing the same thing. I just felt that I needed to stay focused and stay out of trouble.

Diane Lane

The whole chameleon thing about acting. That's why I'm moving towards directing - it's a much more healthy occupation.

Andy Serkis

And what I liked the most about any project was that when it was good, you had a bunch of people trying to accomplish something together who were all acting together as one - that's the most exciting time for me.

Liza Minnelli

If you play it safe every time, then you're missing the best part of acting. You haven't learned anything about your humanity.

Brit Marling

There is something about acting that's mysterious and magical because there is only so much I can do to prepare, and then I have to just let go and breathe and believe that it will come through.

Lupita Nyong'o

Music is my first love and the thing that I feel extremely connected to. I feel like I still have a long way to go within that in terms of being able to perform and write songs. But, yeah, I really hope 'The Possession' opens doors for me to do more acting, because I really enjoyed it.

Matisyahu

The minute I get a big head and start acting like the big man on campus, it's all downhill from there.

Scotty McCreery

Drama is easier to do because you just have to have the emotion and not get caught acting, but comedy is much harder.

Patrick Dempsey

It's fun to look at people that are so good at acting that aren't actors, like David Bowie creating a mystique about rock n' roll. I've listened to 'Ziggy Stardust' as much as any rock n' roll fan - I don't really know what it's about, but it sure is fun to think about David Bowie as this mad creation.

Val Kilmer

And film acting is incredibly tedious, just by its nature. It's incredibly, mind numbingly slow.

Hugh Grant

I really love to act; I love everything about it. I've never had this addiction to being known. I mean, sure, if you go into acting, there's part of you that is saying, 'I want attention' but I was brought up to work to deserve attention, and it is the work, not the trappings that are important.

Christopher Meloni

My personal advice is to go to school first and get a liberal arts education, and then if you want to pursue acting, go to graduate school.

Jillian Bach

The really best acting is children in a playground or in a backyard. They're just lost in their imagination. The backyard isn't a pirate ship or a jungle, in the same way that the soundstage isn't Shambala.

Nolan North

I think by eighth grade I knew I wanted to be an actor. I'd done church plays and stuff, but my first actual acting class was in eighth grade. I was obsessed with it.

Aaron Paul

Acting is glamour but writing is hard work, so I'm going to be an actress.

Jacqueline Susann

Acting is so exciting to me. It's a thrill; otherwise I wouldn't do it. Not to be hokey, but I think life is definitely worth living, whether you're working or not. For an actor, the character is the thing... it doesn't matter what medium you're in. as long as you have something to do.

Elizabeth Mitchell

The only thing of value I have in this life is my ability to tell a story, whether in print, orating, writing it down or having people acting it out. That's why I'm always hoping society never collapses because the first ones to go will be entertainers.

Kevin Smith

You get money out of acting. You get gray hair out of directing. Actually, I get more of a rush from directing.

Tim Robbins

I have had a very physical acting career, but on 'Newsroom,' it's not about physicality, but it's about presence. I get to just be. Strong, sensitive, quiet strength can be much more intimidating than the screaming loud guy, and I'm so glad to get to show this side of me, which, to be honest, is a lot like who I really am.

Terry Crews

To be honest, I never went to school for acting, and I never learned to break down a script. I took acting classes my whole life, but they never taught me anything about acting. They just taught me about myself.

Shailene Woodley

Many reality shows have failed because everyone's acting.

Nigel Barker

After the brain tumor happened, I realized I love acting, I've always loved it, I may never get a chance to do it again.

Mark Ruffalo

Being at the mercy of the acting profession, in the early days of one's career, is really brutal and feels like you have no control over your life, at all.

Charlie Hunnam

I don't care about my personal acting career anymore. I'm done with it. After 10 years of making movies and doing better than I ever could have imagined, I sort of had to ask myself: 'What am I supposed to do with all of this success that I have had?'

Kevin Spacey

Everyone seems to think they know what acting techniques are. Techniques just help you get to a certain place, but if the thing is happening just by itself, you don't need those techniques.

Richard Gere

My goal was for acting to become my main income. I would say to myself, 'I'm good enough.' That became my mantra.

Michael Fassbender

I've always wanted to be an actor. I've never planned on the acting and the stand-up feeding each other; they've always been separate desires.

Jim Gaffigan

What you wear for work should be comfortable and empowering. If you're working in business, your outfit should mean business. If I go to meet somebody about an acting job, or something creative, then I'll be in my jeans. For me, overdressing is my biggest fear.

Twiggy

I love acting. When I'm acting I feel like I'm on vacation. I'm just having a wonderful time. The nightmare is just getting the work to happen.

Elizabeth Pena

I was an amazing bartender and a great waiter. I think, in a way, that was my acting school.

Nick Frost

Acting is all about timing. I mean, who has better timing than the MCs?

Coolio

None of the characters I've played are really like me. That would be boring. That wouldn't be acting.

Anna Paquin

Although it has been said by men of more wit than wisdom, and perhaps more malice than either, that women are naturally incapable of acting prudently, or that they are necessarily determined to folly, I must by no means grant it.

Mary Astell

Acting can be a really silly thing. It's like playing dress-up.

Paul Giamatti

I love acting. I do it as a hobby. If I was able to have that as a career... Hopefully the fashion thing is a stepping-stone. I was so worried when I started modeling that it would hinder my chances of acting.

Cara Delevingne

I was a very good girl for a long time, that's what really drew me to acting. The stage was the perfect place to be outrageous, to be sad, to be angry, to be all these different things.

Joan Allen

The camera does not like acting. The camera is only interested in filming behaviour. So you damn well learn your lines until you know them inside out, while standing on your head!

Ben Kingsley

That's what acting is. You're pretending to be someone else.

Saoirse Ronan

It's always fun messing around with costumes and stuff. You know there is an element of acting that you've got to dress-up; that's part of it.

Gina Bellman

Sometimes fake laughing is hard once you've done a scene 18 times. I don't want to brag, but I have a reputation for being very, very good at that. It's funny finding what's challenging about acting as you go.

Allison Williams

Some people said my acting was a cross between Euell Gibbons, Rodney Allen Rippy and Sheena, Queen of the Jungle.

Wolfman Jack

I hope to make acting my career for the rest of my life, if I can.

Chloe Grace Moretz

Whether I'm acting or making it, at the end of the day it's telling the story; action, drama. You want the audience to feel it - the story, the action, the scene, or a particular shot. I just keep working on crafting my art, on how to make action movies.

Donnie Yen

Drama school is fundamentally practical. I didn't write any essays, so I came out with a BA honors degree in acting.

Emilia Clarke

Acting is a way of living out one's insanity.

Isabelle Huppert

81

Funnily enough, when I was leaving school and they asked you what you were going to do, and I just liked acting, that's never what I would say. I would always say I would go into business, even though I didn't really know what was meant by that.

Kylie Minogue

When I was a little girl, I loved monkeys. I wanted to be a primatologist. I went to the careers office to ask how. Because nobody could give me a good answer, I opted for acting.

Audrey Tautou

Acting is not about dressing up. Acting is about stripping bare. The whole essence of learning lines is to forget them so you can make them sound like you thought of them that instant.

Glenda Jackson

It's what still excites me most about acting: letting your imagination go places it's never been before. There's nothing better than that.

Robin Wright

I don't think I was fully satisfied acting. You know, the girlfriend role or the best friend role, and that wasn't enough for me.

Joey Lauren Adams

There was a lot of dancing in '76, '78, in the '80s. A lot of dancing. The burn years. A lot of dancing. And for a while, working fit in with all that. 'Moonlighting' - that wasn't acting. It was people telling me 'Let's create a character who is you, so you can play him the way you are. The guy you are at night.' It was fun.

Bruce Willis

I love acting because you don't have to do the same thing over and over again, every day, and that's what attracted me to wanting to do this for a living. So to be given an opportunity to create something completely different and live that out is the dream. It's incredibly rewarding.

Jennifer Morrison

To be in front of an audience and pretending, and to lie, this is the principle of acting.

Roberto Benigni

When I'm not acting, I'm at the beach. I like to spend a lot of time in the water, surfing.

Brenton Thwaites

I never lost my appetite for acting.

Eli Wallach

A live performance is the same no matter what genre it is. Wrestling, rock 'n roll, hosting, acting - it's the same thing.

Chris Jericho

Because acting was my only professional outlet, I put a ton of pressure on the roles that I did. I overstepped my bounds, I tried to control things that were out of my purview as an actor and in some cases even tried to direct my scenes because I felt I knew how they should run rather than trust the director.

James Franco

I needed an outlet in high school and came across painting. I've actually been painting longer than I've been acting. A movie is a collaborative effort, and with painting you just have yourself.

James Franco

School allowed me to have outlets so that some of the pressure was taken off the acting. Every role in every movie, I used to live or die by. Once I had these new outlets, I relaxed a lot more.

James Franco

As an actress I find the most enjoyable part of acting is really just to please the director. I just want to please my director.

Joan Chen

I recommend doing some sort of acting class, something that can eventually get you in front of an agent or a manager, and practice is very important.

Bridgit Mendler

I've never cared for the idea of a career path, or where a film might 'take me.' My love is for acting not money, so I only take on roles that I find challenging, in stories I find interesting.

Gael Garcia Bernal

If you go into a bank or a shop and you want them to believe that you're going to shoot them, that's an acting exercise. If you want to turn to someone else who's as tooled up as you are and persuade them to put their knife down because you'll use your knife, that's an acting exercise. Nine out of 10 delinquents are frustrated actors.

Peter Mullan

I was going to say that writing is about disclosure and acting is about obfuscation, but that's such a little lie. Both of them are about obfuscation and masking oneself.

David Rakoff

This acting's serious! And I really respect those actors. It's a tough business to be able to be something you're not and be natural and convince people on camera.

Michael Strahan

The acting part of me is not me. The music side is who I really am and what I want to talk about. It'll be hard for people to differentiate those different sides but I think it's possible. Once the music is out there, people will start to realize how serious I am about it rather than, 'Oh god, another actress making an album.'

Lucy Hale

I always had a separate life than just my work. I built my own family. I have my own hobbies and interests. I have a ranch with livestock and horses. I didn't always get my self-esteem and identity from acting. I never worked unless I wanted to. I never did anything just to do it, just for the paycheck. I always did things that I liked.

Ricky Schroder

I've certainly had less practice at fatherhood than I have at acting, but in fatherhood, at least my failures are private!

Rich Sommer

A producer has to know all about everything from set-building to costumes to acting.

Alan Ladd

My work requires acting at its most committed - it demands actors of enormous resilience, but also intelligence and wit. It doesn't work for narcissistic or selfish actors.

Mike Leigh

About 10,000 years ago, males and females were acting equitably and were treating one another as equals, and then males took over the power, because they have physical power and physical strength.

Jane Elliot

Yes, years of compromise and disappointment have added depth to my acting.

Rufus Sewell

I have only one rule in acting - trust the director and give him heart and soul.

Ava Gardner

I went to performing arts high school, and I took dance and acting every day. Then, I went to Marymount Manhattan College and I have a B.A. in acting, with a concentration in theater performance and a minor in musical theater. I studied there for three years.

Jenna Ushkowitz

I am always acting, be at a party, at work or in office. My attitude changes from meeting to meeting, from being serious to intense to funny, depending on who is in the room.

Karan Johar

I think sometimes soap acting gets an unfair label for being bad and over the top. The lessons I learned there were so valuable. Seeing yourself every day on television, you learned what worked and didn't work, what was bad acting and what wasn't. Memorizing scripts became second nature.

Dylan Bruce

My friends started having children after college, while I was pursuing this crazy acting career and living hand to mouth. Plus, all my boyfriends were artists struggling to make a living. Having kids didn't make any sense - why would I take on more of a financial burden when I couldn't even afford a dog?

Edie Falco

Nothing is better than showing up twice a week, acting like a 12 year-old for two hours, and then going home.

Reid Scott

I live my life with positivity, so even if there was a low, I'd find a positive in the situation. It's how I am with everything in life. With acting, I don't love the celebrity side of it and the tabloids, but at the end of the day, I love what I do so much, it overrides all that.

Hayley Hasselhoff

My mum thought my TV and film addiction was laziness. If you're an immigrant, you know you'll never be an accepted part of society, but you hope your children will be, and you try to make them essential to the community in a practical way - being a doctor or a lawyer. Acting was beyond their comprehension.

Sanjeev Bhaskar

You know, I don't support esoteric approaches to acting.

Christoph Waltz

I'm eternally grateful for the fact that I'm doing what I like best. I thank my stars for it. I wonder why I wasted all that time being fat. I should have lost weight and started acting earlier. But as they say, things happen when they are meant to.

Sonakshi Sinha

Being an actress isn't as fun as it may seem. If I don't love something, I stop doing it. I don't love acting anymore, so I've stopped doing it.

Amanda Bynes

I was born in the '60s and grew up in the '70s - not exactly the best decade for food in British history. It was horrendous. It was a time when, as a nation, we excelled in art and music and acting and photography and fashion - all creative skills... all apart from cooking.

Heston Blumenthal

Then in college, besides economics, I also majored in studio art and got involved in photography and making short films and acting. But I didn't know you could make a living that way.

Brit Marling

I'm lucky because my two best friends are from kindergarten so they never thought that it was a big deal that I was in acting; they don't even ever talk about it. They still act all confused, like, 'What's going on?' when we go places and people come up to me.

Miranda Cosgrove

At this point, I've really failed at a lot of things. It's nice to be able to say that, in a way. I've failed at music. I've failed at dance. And acting - there have been times when I went out and read lines to audition for acting parts. I believe that if anybody wrangled together those audition tapes, it would be pretty hysterically funny.

Steve-O

There is this immediate connection, this intimacy when you're acting because there's no room to be polite or shy. Also, as an actor I get to connect with women I've never met before.

Jessica Chastain

After 'The Real Thing,' I thought about giving up acting because it's difficult to have a rich life outside your work when you're an actress, a private life that can survive being picked up and put down. That's what I thought, anyway.

Jennifer Ehle

What I love about acting is that you are exposed to so many different things. Horse-riding, sailing, travelling to amazing places.

Nikolaj Coster-Waldau

As long as I am acting, I will do only Telugu films. I want to take Telugu films to the world. Everyone should talk about our films.

Mahesh Babu

I directed my first music video for Sara Bareilles. I like writing and directing. I co-wrote '21 Jump Street' and I'm in that. To me, they all inform the other one. I think writing makes you a better actor, acting makes you a better writer, directing makes you better at both. To me, I'm just trying to learn as much as possible.

Jonah Hill

I think this movie, 'Moneyball,' symbolizes becoming a man for me, and I think my character becomes a man. It's important to me: I'm becoming a man. I'm taking my life seriously. I'm taking my acting really seriously, and it's important for me to play adults. It's important for me to change and develop as I get older.

Jonah Hill

The atheist is cheating whenever he makes a moral judgment, acting as though it has an objective reference, when his philosophy in fact precludes it.

William A. Dembski

I don't think I know enough about acting to direct. You need to be a slight megalomaniac, not where you want to take over the world, but where you want to make every single decision and the buck stops with you. It's an awful lot of stress.

Matthew Goode

They say making laws is like making sausages. You shouldn't watch. It's the same for acting, especially for the actor who works unconsciously.

Ed Asner

My whole thing is I want to have a backup plan because maybe I won't get another acting job after 'Fame', maybe I'll want to give up on acting in five years or whatever and I want to have something else that I enjoy just as much as I enjoy acting.

Kay Panabaker

When I used to wrestle professionally, I preferred being the bad guy known as 'The Heel;' you would get to 'work the crowd,' getting them to hate you and want to see you lose, while the good guy 'Babyface' would walk in, smile and shake hands with a few kids, and his acting job was done.

Conan Stevens

When I was in my teens, I thought, 'Would I like to try and work hard at being an actor, or do I want to work hard at doing something musical?' Acting won out, but I do really enjoy those moments where I get to just belt something out.

Emilia Clarke

It's a fine line of doing what's good for your life and what your parents want you to do, but also following your dreams. With my parents, when I was younger, I always had to do two things. If I was acting, I always had to do a sport or something on the arts side of things along with that.

Kaley Cuoco

Acting is a tough business, and the percentage of people who make it is very low - it's about 1 percent.

Lee Majors

Here is something no real celebrity will ever tell you: film acting is not very fun. Doing the same thing over and over again until, in the director's eyes, you 'get it right' does not allow for very much creative freedom... In terms of sheer adrenaline, film has absolutely nothing on theater.

Mara Wilson

I was a swimsuit model, and I got bored. Acting was challenging. It was very hard and intimidating. We choose to do things in life sometimes that scare the crap outta us. Performing in front of people was my challenge.

Christa Campbell

I love being creative. I love acting, but I also love directing because you get to have a vision for the whole and bring that vision to fruition.

Juliet Landau

I think with improv - and I say it all the time because it's become such a catch thing that you talk about improv - if the scene is well-written, you don't need to improv. But that being said, if something strikes you in the moment and, most importantly, you know where the scene is supposed to go, it's no different than method acting.

Vince Vaughn

I think if you're half-hearted you shouldn't go into acting.

Jane Badler

Acting is sort of an extension of childhood. You get to play all of these roles and have so much fun. Playing an athlete would be so cool. Or where you get to shoot guns, ride horses. I wouldn't turn down any of that.

Jon Hamm

I like acting better than anything else, but, you know, directing's good.

Tommy Wiseau

I don't mean to sound - I don't want it to come out funny, but I don't like show business. I love - I love acting in films. I love it.

Gene Wilder

Believe it or not, I kind of went into professional wrestling so I could get an avenue into acting.

Kurt Angle

I did this class when I first moved to California. It was a 'Kids on Camera' class up in the Bay Area. That was good for just getting me excited in acting and everything. Then once I started working down L.A., I just stuck to my acting coach, and she helps me prepare with auditions and that sort of thing.

Bridgit Mendler

Acting is easy and fun. You earn a lot of money, and you bang out with girls. The profession is given tremendous significance within our society, but it's not really worthy of it.

James Spader

Acting is fun and I refuse to get involved in the semantics and the politics of strategy and breaking out of something or doing something because you need to do something else. For me it's all about what fuels my soul and if I'm passionate about a screenplay then that's what I'll do next.

Shailene Woodley

When I started acting, my parents gave me three rules: I had to stay good in school, stay the kid they always knew I was, and I had to have fun. If I wasn't doing those three things, then I couldn't do acting anymore.

Shailene Woodley

The interesting thing about acting is using all your own stuff and having some kind of personal catharsis while you're working.

Melanie Lynskey

I hadn't done just a straight-out comedy in a long time, just letting an ensemble do really good character acting, having them carry the movie as in my earlier pictures.

Brian De Palma

Acting is all about finding the truth within whatever world you're in.

Karen Gillan

My interest in acting came from seeing Broadway shows on summer trips to New York as a child. It was the original production of 'A Chorus Line' in an easy tie with the first 10 -15 minutes of Dustin Hoffman in 'Tootsie' that hooked me on the romantic idea that the impossible, difficult life of a struggling actor was for me.

John Lloyd Young

I have learned a lot from jazz. I compare good acting to jazz music. The more you study and prepare as an actor, the more equipped you are to live in the moment. Just like the gifted musicians in my dad's quartet, it takes a courageous actor to be free.

Nat Wolff

Getting a role in 'Harry Potter' was like winning the lottery. But no one deserves an acting job.

Jessie Cave

I learned mime back when I was in college, at Ball State University, Indiana. That woke up my body from the neck down and made me realize that acting and communication - portraying a story, event, or emotion - is a full-body experience.

Doug Jones

I still have the desire to do the job of acting. It's just a matter of whether I'll be allowed to do the job of acting that remains to be seen. There are only so many brick walls that I'm willing to beat my head on.

Gary Coleman

I'm an entertainer, so in whatever form I entertain... The thing about being a rapper is that you have more control over your form, whereas with acting you have to compromise a lot.

Method Man

I'm a regular Canadian girl. I enjoy staying home. In the summer I've got a garden. I'm very much a homebody, a normal, family-oriented girl. But I do have this other incredible side of my life that involves acting and traveling.

Elisha Cuthbert

Singing is the rawest thing. Having been naked in films or naked in photo shoots, it's nothing compared to singing. It's absolute nakedness. You are stripped bare! It's very strange. Acting seems much easier, in fact, because you are putting on a costume - whereas here, you are taking everything off.

Lou Doillon

Hollywood was a detour, although my mother was an aristocrat from Tokyo who ran away to join the theatre, so acting is in my genes.

Cary-Hiroyuki Tagawa

I learned that the majority of the time, simplicity is the best way to go about things as you peel away the layers... that's when you start finding the gold... I can't say that was from my own acting. That was from observing actors like John Spencer and Martin Sheen... I had a chance just to observe.

Dule Hill

There are plenty of actors who've caught the singing bug and vice versa, but with musical performers, you're constantly a persona - which is something I love about acting: you play a character, you leave and you get to be yourself again.

Freddie Stroma

I think having children in general is always very helpful for acting.

Josh Hamilton

Every acting gig isn't the same, every writing job isn't the same, every live performance isn't the same - the challenge is the level of difficulty or ease, and that may vary.

Ricky Jay

So when I told my parents I wanted to go into acting because I was flunking out of my first year of junior college, they were relieved that I had picked something other than joining the army. But I can't imagine how they had high hopes for me.

Dustin Hoffman

I'm not giving up acting, I'm definitely not going to stop.

Shane West

For a while, I couldn't decide whether or not I should pursue singing in the opera or acting. And I'm glad that I chose the latter because I wasn't a very good singer.

Christoph Waltz

It's different being a director. I suppose, especially if it's a story you've written and you feel compelled to tell, in some ways it's a lot easier than acting because you're orchestrating the piece. As an actor, sometimes you're trying to second-guess what people want.

Paddy Considine

This city can be kind of brutal, so you see your dreams from every different angle, but ultimately it's about acting and if you enjoy acting, you will always enjoy acting.

Radha Mitchell

For me, to be perfectly honest, the part of my brain that was stimulated by directing was much more exciting than a typical day of acting.

Misha Collins

A dream my girlfriend and I have is to move to New York for a year or two because we just love the city. I would take some acting classes.

Daniel Bruhl

Acting has always been a passion of mine, so any opportunity that allows me to do that is definitely of interest to me.

Nick Jonas

Next to acting, being in the great outdoors is my biggest passion.

Seth Numrich

No acting, no production, could take the place of that moment when you come out in the dark on to the stage and the drummer plays four beats on the hi-hat and then lights and music. It just takes your breath away. No words can do what music can.

Ken Stott

I've always been in school plays and performing monologues and taking drama. Now I'm in acting classes. I do it the real way. I want to be a working actor. I would love that. I just like being on a series and having a script, and I want that to be my nine-to-five.

Vinny Guadagnino

I can walk into a room and create a good ambience. I was taught all about this back when I studied acting. One of the things they would teach you is how to send out positive signals when you enter a room. I am glad I learned this.

Jean Reno

Acting is what I love. I love being the chameleon, and you can't do that if you have just one physical type.

Alexander Ludwig

Acting for me was hard enough without having to think of the accent. And also, when I was auditioning for stuff I would walk into the room with an Australian accent ,and I would do the audition in an American accent, and they would invariably say, 'Yeah, it's that good, but I can still hear the oddity coming through.'

Jonathan LaPaglia

I love to see the smiles on people's faces when you cook for them. I love to go to different restaurants. I want to cook because I know this acting isn't going to last forever, and I want something to fall back on. It's another way to make people smile.

Raven-Symone

Quite honestly I never had a desire to be an actor. I tell people, I did not choose acting; acting chose me. I never grew up wanting to be an actor. I wanted to play football. In about 9th grade an English teacher told me I had a talent to act. He said I should audition for a performing arts high school so I did on a whim. I got accepted.

Ving Rhames

Acting is a great way to make a living, especially when I consider what my alternatives were and probably still are. I mean, you are only making movies. It is a lot less pressure than being a surgeon; although it seemed like the only other thing that I was qualified for was manual labour.

James Spader

That's what I love about acting. There's never a set role. You can be a firefighter, you can be a baseball player, you can be whatever you want in the acting world. I think I've found my calling.

Ryan Guzman

Acting with Denzel is like playing tennis with someone that's better than you. You either play better tennis or get blown off the court.

Dean Cain

There's no great mystery to acting. It's a very simple thing to do but you have to work hard at it. It's about asking questions and using your imagination.

Eddie Marsan

When you start so young working, you build a hunger for acting, working, and a busy life.

Bonnie Wright

With acting, I've got a character to inhabit. You've got to think about your intentions and your directions. In modeling, even though there's an act to it, a good model is a good model. For me it's uncomfortable territory. You start to feel quite insecure about yourself. There's nothing between you and the camera, and it's just you.

Max Irons

I agree with Marjorie Rosen's good psychological analysis of my acting ability.

Pola Negri

When I was in high school, I would perform every year in those plays and there was something I really loved about it. But I was completely unaware that you could sort of get into an acting career.

Nick Offerman

I didn't want to be the archetypal sponging brother-in-law, so I didn't go into acting when I got to the States. I thought, 'No, I'll go to school and then I'll be an English teacher; that'll be fun.' But I was horrible as a teacher. As hard as I tried, I just couldn't inspire those kids to take an interest in Milton and Shakespeare and Donne.

John Mahoney

My first acting job - I used to do commercials, and I had done a couple music videos - but my first job job was 'ATL' with T.I. I auditioned for that, like, five times. I didn't have an agent. And then, from there, my life changed.

Lauren London

It was only after university that I said to myself that I had to take the risk and have a serious go at acting. It's such a bizarre profession, because you have to be totally tough to deal with all those times when you're being turned down, and then really soft in order to access your character's emotions.

Felicity Jones

There's something about being any kind of entertainer that is acting. You have to put on a show. Things you wouldn't do in your life, you do on stage. You have to let go. And that's extra hard for rappers. We have a tendency to, quote unquote, keep it real. As an actor, you have to be able to humiliate yourself. Do whatever it takes.

Heavy D

It all started in Michigan. My dad got a job in Michigan, so we all moved up there from St. Louis. I kind of hung out in the summer and had nothing to do, so I sort of got into acting. And then I was going to Grand Blanc High, doing the acting thing and hoping it would pan out.

Evan Peters

I always stayed for the first curtain call and people always said, 'Who's that?' But this got me started in acting.

James Stewart

I don't find acting to be a particularly noble way to make a living. I'm not saving anybody's life, I'm not a teacher, I'm not working for UNICEF. I don't think I'm some big deal.

Ellen Pompeo

I was a terrific liar as a child, and I believe my lies. So it's a natural step into acting.

Anthony Geary

I miss the physicality of drumming. There's immediateness about it that I'm always striving for in my acting. Maybe I'm in the wrong profession. I certainly wish I could spend more time pursuing music. It feels like a part of me I'm neglecting.

Trevor St. John

I was never a villain on the stage. I always played strong, sympathetic types. My first stage role with a speaking part, believe it or not, was as a priest. It wasn't until I began acting in films that the producers and directors saw me primarily as a bizarre villain.

Conrad Veidt

Singing is an incredible expression and something that is important to me, but where I feel comfortable with how much I reveal about myself is acting. I enjoy the characters, the costumes, the wigs and just being a chameleon.

Brie Larson

To be an actress and act crazy is really fun for me, to be able to be acting like you'd never be able to act in your real life and scream and freak out. It's an interesting test for an actor.

Alexandra Daddario

During my senior year, I was supposed to spend a semester student teaching, but decided I couldn't be a teacher. My aunt Beth's friend was Jackie Gleason's daughter, Linda Miller. She encouraged me to talk to her. After doing that, she recommended Catholic University's M.F.A. acting program. So that's what I did.

Siobhan Fallon Hogan

My favorite way of getting out of doing chores is by acting like I'm asleep. But it never works.

Devon Werkheiser

There's a oneness to showing yourself to an audience. They feel that. It's healthy. That's what acting is all about.

Catherine Hicks

Acting for me is like a ping-pong game. That's the secret of acting. When you have a really good actor, I always want to be as good as he is or she is.

Sibel Kekilli

In my opinion, the actors I admire the most are also character actors - the Dustin Hoffmans and the Robert De Niros. You look at them from film to film, and there's clearly more going on than just the repeat of the same persona over and over again. They find characters, and they submerge themselves. I think good acting is always character acting.

William Sadler

There's a Zen to acting, by being in the moment. That's where the power is.

Christine Ebersole

It's nice to have my mother as someone I can talk to about acting. My dad's a director, so when he comes to watch me on set, he think it's his set. He's always telling a production assistant, 'Can you get me five donuts?'

Zoey Deutch

That's a tough question; I've been acting since I was 10. My dad was an entrepreneur, so I guess something along those lines. I wouldn't want a 9-5 job.

Will Estes

There will be times when you just can't seem to land an acting job, and you feel like giving up. Don't! The only way to realise that dream is to keep working hard for it.

Sam Claflin

I never thought I'd be making a living off of acting - it's still kind of a shock for my family and friends to see my face on TV every Wednesday night.

Matthew Gray Gubler

We believe, in fact, that the one act of respect has little force unless matched by the other - in balance with it... The acting out of that dual respect I would name as precisely the source of our power.

Barbara Deming

Acting is such a crazy industry, but kite boarding keeps me grounded.

Maika Monroe

I would say that 'Shake It Up' was a chance for me to do two things I really love: acting and dancing.

Zendaya

The post-'Merlin' era is an exciting time to look forward to. Variety is the spice of life. That's the fantastic thing about acting - all the different challenges it can provide you with. To limit yourself just to one would be foolish; therefore, I'm looking forward to different things that come my way.

Bradley James

The art of acting consists in keeping people from coughing.

Ralph Richardson

It was a lot of fun being a child actress. It suited me. I don't think it suits everybody, but I was in it because I had a passion, not because my parents wanted me to make money. If other kids want to do it, and they really like acting, go for it.

Alanna Ubach

For me, I need to be able to show up on set and fart around and goof around. If I can have that, when I'm not acting, then when I'm acting I can go however deep and dark and bad I need to. I developed that more with 'Breaking Bad' because I've never worked on anything as dark for as long.

Betsy Brandt

I was a very determined kid. I couldn't imagine any other life for myself. This happens to kids who are different in any way. How am

I going to make a life? Who am I going to be when I grow up? Will there be a place for me in the world? Acting gave me a sense of purpose, but it also gave me a sense that I would survive, that I would find my place.

Linda Hunt

I don't take acting classes - I'm quite an autodidact. I prefer to learn from other actors by watching various movies. Evaluate my acting, spot the flaws and fix them.

Joe Taslim

Directing is a lot of fun, but you have to be on your toes every minute. If you zone out for even a second, you'll miss something and things will get screwed up. And here's a little secret that I'm going to let out of the bag: That is not the case with acting.

Misha Collins

When I work on a movie, I never aim for records, collections or the number one position. I always concentrate on my work and look for ways to improve my acting abilities. I also advise my co-stars not to concentrate on these pretty issues and just focus on acting.

Mahesh Babu

I really started dreaming... and broke out of my shyness when I got to Howard University. My first acting class was an Intro to Acting class with Professor Bay, who really broke me out of my shell, encouraged me to follow my dreams and make them a reality.

Lance Gross

Hollywood is fickle; your career can end pretty fast. If the acting jobs dry up, you have to have something to fall back on. In fact, that would be my advice to kids interested in acting - make sure you get an education too.

Matthew Lawrence

When you're acting, you're a person. When you're modeling, you're a hanger.

Analeigh Tipton

The first acting thing I ever did was my senior year I decided not to play a sport in the Spring and, in that Spring B.J. Novak who went to school with me, asked if I'd be in this show that was a parody of all the teachers in the school, 'sure!' That was the first acting thing I did.

John Krasinski

I'm an actor. If you had said to me before I started acting that I'd get two bites of the cherry - you would do things that people will remember forever like 'The Brothers' which I did in the '70s and now 'Doctor Who' - I'd have been overjoyed and I still am.

Colin Baker

Auditioning and actually acting on a set are two different things. When you audition, you're in a room and you don't have anything to play with and you don't have anything physically in the room. Whereas on set, you have direction, you have costumes, and you have other actors to work with. It's a completely different thing.

Adelaide Kane

I'm terrified of being too famous. What I'm really afraid of is that the audiences will go into the theater and not be able to forget that it's me, that fame will stand in the way of my acting. I want to keep being able to change into different shapes and different personalities.

Noomi Rapace

I am a soldier, convinced that I am acting on behalf of soldiers.

Siegfried Sassoon

Acting is like a sporting match; a tennis game, but no one should win or lose. The game's the thing!

Jon Polito

I didn't want to be famous. I just wanted to earn enough money to have a nice life and enjoy acting.

David McCallum

'Everwood' I think provides a unique feeling, an emotional experience. And other shows on TV don't have the acting talent to do that. Each one of our actors can do a serious scene and a humorous scene, and can do it all within the same sequence. They can go from a heartbreaking moment to a humorous moment.

Greg Berlanti

What I would say to a person who is firm in their faith and wants to go into an acting career: It is such a difficult thing to do without compromising your beliefs.

Angus T. Jones

Part of the reason why I love acting is that you do hope that somehow your work will connect to people and somehow expand their consciousness somewhat, and being able to challenge notions of prejudice through work - through my work - is really thrilling.

Gwendoline Christie

My best friend growing up really put the bug in my ear about acting. We created this one hour-and-a-half improv play when we were 10 or 11 and performed it at the library. We just played off each other so well and had the best time doing it and the funniest part was, we wound up having packed houses, other people loved it too.

Katherine Moennig

I see all these people talking about acting as a great spiritual thing. It's not. There's no great mystery to acting. It's a very simple thing to do, but you have to work hard at it. It's about asking questions and using your imagination.

Eddie Marsan

I have these surreal moments where I'm like, 'I'm pregnant with Jake Gyllenhaal's baby' and 'I'm telling Robert Pattinson that he smells of sex.' But you're acting, so the focus is on the work.

Sarah Gadon

To me, acting is acting... I'd be happy working on a street corner in a mime troupe.

Kelly McGillis

Just to get a job is always really exciting to me. I do feel there's a lot left for me to learn about movies, the subtleties of acting.

Sebastian Stan

The idea of transformation - playing something I'm not - is the bit I enjoy most about acting.

Mark Strong

I still don't know what I'm going to be. I love acting. I would love to be an English teacher. I would love to be a housewife and have a chateau in the South of France, I would love to be a singer that travels to cafes around different towns.

Bethany Joy Lenz

I grew up in St. Louis, Missouri. I lived in Grand Blanc, Michigan for a year and that's when I got involved in acting and took classes there. A manager who saw me at the agency I was at in Michigan wanted me to come out to L.A.

Evan Peters

Before I ever had the idea of becoming an actor, or ever picking up a guitar or listening to classic rock or anything like that, I was an artist. I used to draw and paint all the time. So I've always been very artistic, and I always will be. So art in general - music, acting, performing, painting, drawing, everything - I'm very passionate about it.

Billy Unger

I never went to acting school. I started in the circus, music hall, I was in a group, did kids' bits. I've always had this kind of insecurity being uneducated.

Rupert Graves

I went to a dentist for a toothache, and it turned out his kids were in an acting school. We talked about it, and I decided to enroll at the same school. I was 14. I guess you could say I just got lucky.

Nolan Gerard Funk

I know what it's like to have a dream. I know what it's like to roll the dice and say, 'I'm going to go after this thing,' and nothing turns my stomach quicker than acting teachers or acting schools that look at a bunch of dreamers and say, 'We can help,' when they know full well that they can't.

Jim Parrack

I like to act. I guess letting what you love be what you do is key. I've worked very hard for that to be the case, probably because I'm very lazy and I only want to do things that are fun and I run away from anything that feels like work... Acting for me is like lunch at school... you're just in a playground where you get to pretend and play.

Dichen Lachman

I have done so much: modeling, acting, singing, the calendar, the lingerie line, and there have been times where I have wanted to give up but I went for it.

Caprice Bourret

I'm not looking to be a trophy. When not acting, I spend my time studying metaphysics and quantum mechanics to keep my life as grounded as I can.

Tanit Phoenix

The thing about acting is you don't want to let on how enjoyable it is or then everybody would want to become an actress. But it really is. It's a pleasure to go and exchange your identity.

Gena Rowlands

As an actor, you act in order to make a living. Then, when you can make a living, you start acting because you want to do what you love to do. I need to remind myself of that a lot.

Ty Simpkins

I was like the class clown in school so I guess I would say I did like the attention. In church I did a lot of plays, my mother made me play characters, do a lot of drama and acting, trying to become someone else. So it helped me create who I am, to create Snoop Dogg.

Snoop Dogg

Right before I got 'Sons of Anarchy,' I actually quit acting for 18 months and didn't read a single script, and I wrote a film. I felt like I needed to do something that I had control over, as an artist, and also just do something where I felt like I had some control over my life, as just a human, out in the world.

Charlie Hunnam

Stop acting as if life is a rehearsal. Live this day as if it were your last. The past is over and gone. The future is not guaranteed.

Wayne Dyer

I know very little about acting. I'm just an incredibly gifted faker.

Robert Downey, Jr.

I remember my choir teacher in high school told me, 'When in doubt, sing loud.' I'm a terrible singer, but I always auditioned for the musicals, and would get cast in them because I really would just put it all out there. That was really good advice, and I think it works for everything, not just acting.

Judy Greer

Acting is just being a man. Being human. Not forcing it.

Peter O'Toole

Acting is about communicating what it is like to be human: the pain, the laughs, the misery, the joy. I suppose I am searching to have it all.

Rosamund Pike

Justice is rather the activity of truth, than a virtue in itself. Truth tells us what is due to others, and justice renders that due. Injustice is acting a lie.

Horace Walpole

Acting is not about being famous, it's about exploring the human soul.

Annette Bening

No one is truly free, they are a slave to wealth, fortune, the law, or other people restraining them from acting according to their will.

Euripides

I couldn't be 'Johnny' in front of a camera in acting jobs and behind the camera I like to be 'Michael.' With directing, you can't do it by halves. There's a lot of reflection, and I have found that I, as

'Michael,' thrive on it. It's lovely coming home and feeling that stuff from a day's work as myself.

Johnny Vegas

Acting is magical. Change your look and your attitude, and you can be anyone.

Alicia Witt

I recognize that I have a unique position to be a role model to young girls because I am doing something that they consider glamorous, which is acting, and yet I took a time to really get my education and study mathematics, and I think math is the cat's meow.

Danica McKellar

More than anything, acting helped me discover who I'm not. I've learned that I'm a girly girl, but not a prissy girl.

Debby Ryan

I've always wanted to play a spy, because it is the ultimate acting exercise. You are never what you seem.

Benedict Cumberbatch

An unforgettable experience happened on December 15, 1996 when I won the Supermodel contest while still in school. I was just seventeen years old then. Winning that competition was the turning point of my life. That's how I got into modeling and later started acting.

Bipasha Basu

I think acting is about forgetting yourself in order to give the best of yourself. It's passing through you more than you're creating it. You're not the flower, but the vase which holds the flower.

Juliette Binoche

Acting is the expression of a neurotic impulse. It's a bum's life. Quitting acting, that's the sign of maturity.

Marlon Brando

But then acting is all about faking. We're all very good at faking things that we have no competence with.

John Cleese

If you look good, you can act in a Bollywood movie, you don't have to be able to act; and Aishwarya Rai is a great example of this. She is a beautiful woman... You look at her, I want to look at her. Damn, she is fine; but stop acting or stop trying to act.

Russell Peters

Writing is a very strenuous thing - it's like banging your head against a wall. At the end of the day, acting is better, just because nobody ever asked me if I wanted a Pellegrino in the writer's room.

Donald Glover

Plastic surgery and breast implants are fine for people who want that, if it makes them feel better about who they are. But, it makes these people, actors especially, fantasy figures for a fantasy world. Acting is about being real being honest.

Kate Winslet

I've always wanted to get into acting, ever since I was younger. I'd put on shows for my family and run around play dress-up all the time. I think I was 4 when I told them I wanted to do movies.

Emma Roberts

An actor has to be very, very careful, as one of the most wonderful props - and actors love props - is a cigarette. There's so much to do with it: you can bring it up to your face, play with the smoke. It's just the greatest - ever since I was 16 and in acting school in England, I've been playing around with cigarettes.

Melissa Leo

When I look at acting careers that I really admire, I see that it's been a precise decision-making process for these people. They make decisions based on what they love, and they do only the things that they are passionate about. They play only characters that they can't stop thinking about.

Taylor Swift

I injured myself quite badly when I was seventeen. I broke my ankle, and it didn't heal in such a way that I could keep dancing at the level I wanted to. It wasn't like, 'Oh my god, I'll never play the violin again.' I could, but not at the level I wanted. So, I segued into acting, the other thing that was also meaningful to me.

Kristin Lehman

With acting, it's like you form chemistry with different people in different ways, so it's really added even more fun to work, you know?

Tyler Blackburn

The acting bug just seemed to stick with me. I loved going to theatre school in college and continued to train in film classes and had been auditioning for T.V. and movie roles since I was in my late teens. My career has been slow and steady, and I kind of like it that way.

Laura Mennell

My dad was always taking photos of us at home, and even on set - he'd bring us along and stick us in the photos in the background. It was almost the beginning of acting for me, like, 'Hey, you go over there and play basketball in the background, and don't even think about the camera.'

Ansel Elgort

My best advice to actors is if you love acting, do it every chance you get. Success does not mean success. All that matters is whether or not you're doing your best to entertain. The way this business works is all about luck and timing.

Matthew Gray Gubler

Tisch has a great film program and a great acting program, but they are segregated; you don't really intertwine. My peers knew I liked acting, so they'd be like, 'Go get that guy Gubler. He'll be in your student film.' I was in the same building. I became their go-to guy. So I left NYU having been in probably one thousand short films.

Matthew Gray Gubler

On a film, I was always acting. I was either changing my clothes really quickly and wiping off the lipstick and putting on the other lipstick and then working constantly, constantly.

Maggie Gyllenhaal

You have to examine a scene on the page first. Then you get into the basics of acting: Who are you? Who are you talking to? How do you feel about that person?

Debbie Allen

Acting is fantastic, but to be able to create a whole world on celluloid is amazing. It's like taking your dreams straight from your head and projecting them onto a screen.

Amber Benson

Acting is probably the number one team sport in America as far as I'm concerned.

Neal McDonough

Engineers are either aggressive or passive aggressive. You need to just dive straight into it, and sometimes there are social repercussions because of it. The impression that people had of me was that I was really harsh, hard-edged, brusque, and to the point. All of that happened because I am a woman, and I was acting in that kind of environment.

Ruchi Sanghvi

I already have my dream job. Acting was the only thing that ever really kept my attention, and I'm very fortunate that I can have a career doing something I love.

Brant Daugherty

Because Naughty Dog relies on their facial team to hand animate the faces of each game character and they do such a remarkable job, I think you can be more realistic with your acting. It gives the story and what's happening to you the feeling that it's a game.

Nolan North

Acting has been my first passion, and turning a producer was a natural progression.

Riteish Deshmukh

I was the leading star in 1945. I slowed down my pace of acting assignments after I came into direction.

Dev Anand

Acting is our job, not talking about it. In France, they know me like I belong to their family. I go somewhere and I feel like I'm sometimes the aunt, the grandmother, the mother, the sister. They all know me. But it's not supposed to be that way.

Carole Bouquet

'Saturday Night Live' was actually started with a show that Lorne Michaels and I did at a summer camp called Timberlane in Ontario when we were 14 and 15. We would do an improvisational show with music, comedy and acting.

Howard Shore

When I was a kid, I used to pretend to be Bond; I used to make up scenarios and irritate my sister and annoy my mother and father pretending to be someone else, so I kind of was already acting when I was a child. I just didn't really know it.

Aneurin Barnard

I started going to acting school in my senior year in high school, and I remained in acting school through four years of college.

Dane DeHaan

I thought acting was all about natural instinct but I've realised, through working with so many talented actors on 'Wild Swans' and 'Run,' that I can see the training. That's why I am back at drama school.

Katie Leung

I haven't modelled since I was 12 - that was a one-time thing, and I did it as a kid to make a little money to save up for university. Acting is my first love as well as writing and eventually producing and directing.

Kyle Schmid

I live in New York and I love it, because it doesn't make me feel like my life is always just about acting and that world of acting. I don't have expectations.

Sebastian Stan

My mother keeps things in perspective for me. She makes me realize that the acting I do and love is no more important than what one of my brothers does-he works in a shoe repair shop. If my career ever tapers off, I'll go to college.

Dana Hill

The great thing about acting is that, until you're dead, you can do it. There are aspects to it that as time goes on you hope you get better at, and there are a lot of things that I'm excited to explore.

Gil Bellows

Don't let the world define you. In the world of acting, and I think in any profession, really, people are really eager to put you in a box and categorize you as one particular thing.

Jonathan Groff

I also want to get out there in the world and do some acting and fashion and modeling.

Nastia Liukin

A lot of people just look at acting as a quick fix - they don't have a work ethic. This is a job; it's not all margaritas on the beach.

Jeremy Luke

I would be the worst acting coach ever, because I have no idea what I'm doing.

Aaron Douglas

I mean one of the basic rules when you're acting is that you mustn't stand in judgement on a character, you mustn't say Hitler was a bad man because you can't act in that way.

Janet Suzman

Acting has always been a way for me to express the emotions I had buried. If I hadn't acted, I would have gone insane. In my acting class, I could let out my real tears and everyone thought it was the character. But no, it was me.

Tony Leung Chiu-Wai

I want to be able to make people laugh and cry and feel happy or sad and feel all these different emotions through singing and acting. Hopefully throughout my career, I'll get to pursue them.

Olivia Holt

When there wasn't a lot of work, I wrote a screenplay, 'What Lies Beneath,' which got noticed and got me more acting jobs. As I got more jobs, I was able to make my own films. That ethos of making my own work has provided me with a lot of opportunities.

Clark Gregg

With 'Shameless,' 'Homeland' and 'American Horror Story,' these are all shows that don't follow a particular mold, and they are out-there. The acting is spectacular.

Shanola Hampton

Sweden is a small country and, well, our family's pretty prominent in that world, I guess. And I really didn't like the sound of just being 'the fourth acting Skarsgard.'

Bill Skarsgard

I was lucky enough, when I was younger, to have the chance to do as much as possible, and I found what I wanted to do. I did swimming, gymnastics, kickboxing and the one that took off more than the others was acting.

Aaron Johnson

Acting is about giving yourself away, like the U2 song 'With or Without You.' You just don't stay behind a character and make people laugh or cry. At some point you have to take off that mask, and when you do, you're a human being, not just an actor. After all, I'm Catherine the person first. You share that.

Catherine Hicks

I was bullied from grade one to six. Even middle school was tough for me. Everyone had these pre-existing friendships, and I was the new kid, who was acting, so that didn't help much either. It was really tough.

Devon Bostick

You can't think about how people will perceive you or your character. All you can do is focus on your work. The rest is up to the universe. I've been acting for 16 years. I've done 55 movies and, in all seriousness, there's maybe five that are good and the rest are crap.

Robert Patrick

I feel like my music is just an extension of my acting. I treat the songs like scenes that tell a story... it's very similar. My favorite thing is when cartoon fans show up to my live gigs! They are always the most kick-butt audience members 'cause they're not trying to act all cool like a lot of the music fans do! It's refreshing!!

Grey DeLisle

I think the beautiful thing about acting is you don't really know who you are. You're able to be whatever you want any day during the week. So I really couldn't see myself being anything else.

Steven R. McQueen

We on our part will stick to our independent foreign policy of peace, acting forever as a strong defender of world peace and a persistent proponent of common development.

Jinato Hu

I wanted to stay in New York to pursue acting, but my dad urged me to get a four-year degree. Reading about the film school at Florida State University, he suggested I go there. I received my bachelor's degree in 2003.

Lauren Miller

I spent a lot of time taking acting lessons... Actors have no inhibitions, and I'm inhibited by everything. To be able to make fun of yourself is a skill and a liberating experience.

Maksim Chmerkovskiy

From a young age, I had done a lot of theater and musical theater. I wasn't really sure what I wanted to do with my life, but every time I was away from acting, I just felt very incomplete and a little stir crazy.

Alexander Koch

I was changing a light bulb over Groucho Marx's bed, so I took my shoes off, got on his bed and changed the bulb. When I got off the bed he said: 'That's the best acting you've ever done.'

Elliott Gould

I don't like, and I've never been very good at, close-up shots. As soon as you have the camera right there in front of you, it feels like you're in a different reality from the person you are acting with; you lose any real connection with them.

Eve Best

You can count on one hand the white rappers that have made it. So I just wanted to show the point of view of an actor in Hollywood, because what could be more soft than that. Rapping about auditions and acting and stuff. I thought it was just uncharted territory to clown on, so that pushed through with Dirt Nasty.

Simon Rex

I always had a real love of children's presenting, and I was lucky enough to do that and have an acting career alongside it.

Sophie Aldred

I think that in France, we really admire American films, we admire their drive, we admire the modernity and ellipsism in the film and the writing and the style of acting, and we look at them perhaps in a way to see what we can steal from them, too, to make our own films more modern.

Francois Cluzet

There was a period when I really had to ask myself, 'What does acting mean to me?' I'm not someone who's content being famous, with that whole lifestyle. I had to realize I could find a balance between what I like to do and what people think you're 'supposed' to do as an actress.

Lecy Goranson

Being on stage is a seductive lifestyle. My advice to aspiring actors is think twice. People sometimes go into acting for the wrong reasons - as a shortcut to fame and fortune. If these goals are not attained, they feel a bitter disappointment.

Chris Sarandon

When I started acting, I hoped I could make some kind of positive contribution to this world. When I get a letter from some kid in Nebraska saying that, prior to Han, nobody wanted to be his friend because Asians weren't cool if they weren't into martial arts - Now he's accepted and recognized as a human being. That's pretty awesome, right?

Sung Kang

The great thing about acting is that you get to be a lot of different things in one lifetime. You get to explore different personalities and characters.

Eva Amurri

Photography is a hobby born out of my time in undergrad at USC. It is more of a pleasurable hobby, a stress reliever. I don't consider it a professional endeavor like acting or directing.

Lee Thompson Young

I think it's much richer and much more fun to be an artist than to be anything else. I can't think of a better life than acting.

Edward Herrmann

When I started acting, it was like a double identity crisis - your basic crisis, compounded by people saying, 'there goes Robards' kid, Bacall's kid.' Now I realize, sure, that gets your foot in the door, but once it's there, it's your foot. I'm not bothered anymore. I'm confident of my abilities.

Sam Robards

I wasn't really driven to be an actor or anything, but in college I decided to study acting, much to my parents' disappointment. I attended Mason Gross School of the Arts at Rutgers where Bill Esper was, and that is where I really got hooked on the art of acting, and, almost, the chemistry of acting.

Roger Bart

Well I was eight years old, and I have an older cousin who is three years older than me and she was doing acting, commercials, and modeling at the time and... to see my cousin doing that was really inspiring and I wanted to do it. So I went to my mom and I asked her if I could do it, and for the acting part of it, she made me study for a year.

Hailee Steinfeld

With acting, I've always gotten by in life acting in situations. I'm a small person. I didn't have a chance to be a bully. But I could always act myself out of tough situations.

T'Keyah Crystal Keymah

Growing up in this post-apartheid era, the first generation of teens in South Africa living in this new democracy, I often found myself feeling different. I was often the only person of color in an otherwise all-white school. And within the Indian community, because of my training with an English acting teacher, my accent was very different.

Adhir Kalyan

It's important to have a fallback and other activities that keep you interested. I started acting when I was about nine or 10 years old. My father was a midtown firefighter so I always wanted to be a firefighter, but then acting came along. I have to have a plan B.

Jake T. Austin

Acting offers me an outlet. Here is the perfect opportunity to spend fleeting moments becoming an entirely different person; to experience a character entirely unlike myself, but to also make such a character a part of me. There is no routine here; there is no boredom.

Osric Chau

No one will die because of bad acting. No one will die because you missed a cue. We're all human beings. If mistakes are made, you figure out that you're going to live.

Kate Baldwin

Acting classes, I guess, are good and I would like to maybe sometime take one. But I would feel like I was learning someone else's technique. I like mine.

Frankie Muniz

I think everyone should take an acting class. It's like therapy because you get to learn a lot about yourself if it's the right teacher. You're putting yourself up there in front of people, and it takes a lot of the intimidation of everyday away.

Joelle Carter

If I wasn't acting, all I'd do is ride my bike. I've always loved doing that.

Mason Cook

I actually wanted to be a police officer like my dad for the longest time, up until my sophomore year in high school when I started doing plays. I did plays when I was little, but in high school, I started getting into acting.

Chad Lindberg

I decided to take a stab at acting. I entered the American Academy of Dramatic Art, where one teacher told me I'd never make it - I was too tall.

Fred Gwynne

Acting's not particularly complicated. But the great thing is you can step into somebody else's shoes without dealing with the consequences. It's very therapeutic in that way.

Nick Robinson

I'm a bug on acting, which distinguishes Second City from a lot of other revues. It comes from the character, the behavior, and not from the jokes. I don't think jokes are funny. Humor comes out of character and out of situations the character is in.

Bernard Sahlins

All real freedom springs from necessity, for it can be gained only through the exercise of the individual will, and that will can be roused to energetic action only by the force of necessity acting upon it from the outside to spur it to effort.

Anna C. Brackett

I've always loved acting, even from when I was a child. But when I got on stage, I realised I couldn't act my way out of a paper bag. I was wild and full of unharnessed energy, but I was around all these seasoned performers like Rita Cullis. It was as if they were all in slow motion.

Claron McFadden

In my long and difficult and mature life, I have come to learn that the less I know about acting and the more I know about everything else, the better I'll be at both acting and living.

Jean Seberg

I love to cook. I'd have a dinner party, and someone would be like, 'Can you do this at my house?' So my catering partner and I - we were both struggling actresses at the time - thought, instead of getting a waitressing job, let's do what we love. We always said if things pick up, our acting careers come first.

Meta Golding

Acting is an art form. If you are not creating something that's unusual and informative and at least has the possibility of being illuminating, then you are not into it as an art form.

Bruce Glover

I'm from Miami, I love it when we're out in the heat. When it's cold, I'm like, 'I'm never acting again,' because it's too freezing.

Majandra Delfino

I think I had a shyness about me, I think I discovered acting as a way to break out of that and as a way of belonging, a sense of being special.

Michael C. Hall

For me, one of the lessons from 9/11 is that you have to give the organization context for how you're acting, and you've got to communicate constantly, in this case particularly with all the changes that were occurring in the financial marketplace and in the economy.

Kenneth Chenault

Every time I try to retire, or even think of retiring from acting, my agent comes up with a script.

Anthony Hopkins

If I didn't have children I'd be a much better actress. I wouldn't be so distracted. I could pour 100 percent of my energies into it, to promote the investigation which acting is.

Jessica Lange

When I got into the film business, my aim was to adopt a positive persona, of a guy who fights against injustice. And it saved me, because my acting was atrocious to say the least!

Chuck Norris

I just wanted to be a composer; I became an actor by default, really. I got a scholarship to a college of music and drama, hoping to take a scholarship in music. But I ended up as an acting student, so I've stuck with that for the last 50-odd years.

Anthony Hopkins

There's a small percentage of people who can act. There's a small percentage who get to do this for a living. There's a swath of the population that are able to keep a story in their head and fight all the battles against self-consciousness and the surreal unnaturalness of acting in a movie. The technical aspects you can learn fairly quickly.

Tom Hanks

I don't make much distinction between being a stand-up comic and acting Shakespeare - in fact, unless you're a good comedian, you're never going to be able to play Hamlet properly.

Ian Mckellen

If you're trying to learn how to act from a class, you're analyzing the teachers' movements and their intricacies, and it becomes like a pantomime of you wanting to be them, and that's wrong. Literature is an easier way to study acting, because then you can take any kind of spin. It's your own imagination, and your own version of it.

Shia LaBeouf

I got a little house in East L.A. and did the gardening. I was doing some acting here and there, doing my own thing... getting back to reality.

Adam Ant

I would like to continue acting. But also - if this is a dream world where everything could become true - I'd want to be a ballerina.

Elle Fanning

Just the service aspect of running a nonprofit is so gratifying because it takes the attention off yourself. I'm not an acting monk or anything. I'm not, like, the most well-adjusted actor. But it's really designed to focus on yourself, or it can be. So it's good to have something else to focus on that reminds you that it's not always about you.

Adam Driver

To choose ways of not acting was ever the concern and scruple of my life.

Fernando Pessoa

I feel like some of the best talent is on TV right now, with the writing, acting and great directors. I've also been looking for the consistency of work that TV provides for you. And, I always thought it would be really interesting to live with a character for months, if not years.

Christina Ricci

I think in any form of acting, you're always well served if you've done theater.

Jim Parsons

By the end of an intense four years at UCLA, I had co-authored a new math proof, which the media, in fact, loved. As it turned out, math itself blazed my entry back into the spotlight and consequently into wonderful acting jobs like 'The West Wing' and others. You just never know, do you?

Danica McKellar

I like reading novels because it provides insight into human behavior. I am really interested in feelings and think they are what define us as a species. When you really get it right in acting, it's an act of empathy. You feel less distant from others, and that is really exciting.

Claire Danes

Acting is like going to the gym. You have to keep yourself in shape and concentrate on your core.

Anthony Rapp

If laws acting upon private interests can not always be avoided, they should be confined within the narrowest limits, and left wherever possible to the legislatures of the States.

Martin Van Buren

I enjoy doing things that involve research because it's part of what I enjoy about acting.

Michael Sheen

I think things through a lot, so I probably use my head more than my heart. That probably comes through in my acting.

Neil Patrick Harris

I think there is a lot of overexplaining both in writing and acting. People don't need to be hit on the head.

Clive Owen

Both music and acting are huge parts of my life - it's all about balance.

Victoria Justice

Ralph Fiennes was a pivotal influence on me. He asked me, 'So what is it you want to do?' I very shyly, timidly admitted that I wanted to be an actor. He sighed, and he said, 'Lupita, only be an actor if you feel there is nothing else in the world you want to do - only do it if you feel you cannot live without acting.'

Lupita Nyong'o

I've led three lives: the acting part, wife and mother - which is a career - and international relations. I'm proud of my career, the first one, and I'm proud of the other two, too.

Shirley Temple

I love disappearing. That's what acting is. For me it's about putting on a persona, stepping into a pair of shoes. It's my face, but I'm using it as a tool for that spirit, that character.

Sally Hawkins

I'll keep on acting 'til they wipe the drool. I like the business. I like to do different parts and diverse characters. I haven't lost my enthusiasm yet!

Robert Duvall

My mom kind of led me toward acting. She wanted to be an actress when she was younger. That made me interested in it when I was a kid, because she and I are very close.

Stephen Colbert

Something I learned in the Marine Corps that I've applied to acting is, one, taking direction, and then working with a group of people to accomplish a mission and knowing your role within that team.

Adam Driver

Acting, at least for me, is very unreal, and when I'm doing it, I actually feel embarrassed.

Steve Vai

My acting coach I've got here, Richard Lawson, he's been doing good, just telling me to calm down sometimes and just be me.

Kevin Durant

The ultimate acting is to destroy yourself.

Klaus Kinski

I come from the theater and I plan to always do theater. So I don't really see myself not being able to act even if people don't think I am sexy enough for film at 40, I'll still be acting.

Kerry Washington

I'm the artist when I'm doing music that I am when I'm acting. I'm everything.

Eddie Murphy

I don't see myself doing catalog shoots in Madrid anymore like I was doing two years ago. I hope that the acting side of things grows.

Brooklyn Decker

Acting is the physical representation of a mental picture and the projection of an emotional concept.

Laurette Taylor

If you hang around long enough to show these people what you can do, you have a chance in this acting business.

Frank Cady

Acting is not my favourite thing. I don't like wearing costumes and wigs.

Victoria Wood

I have a constant sort of melancholy approach to acting that fuels me. I want to do everything.

Sam Rockwell

My background is a small town with no movie theater. So... I always pictured myself onstage. I went to acting school and learned all the skills. I left early because I did my first movie and discovered that I really loved the minimalistic work with the camera.

Franka Potente

My father loved 'Godard and Truffaut.' He was more artsy. My mom loved the 'Bourne' trilogy; she likes big blockbusters. She loved that I did 'I Am Legend.' My passion for acting came with my passion for movies.

Alice Braga

Acting is such a weird job.

Michael Cera

In searching for a rationale to go to war, Bush settled on the notion of Saddam as an incarnation of evil, basically, and convinced himself that Saddam was fundamentally Adolf Hitler reborn. I think his feelings towards Saddam were in fact quite genuine and quite legitimately hostile. He was not play acting.

Rick Atkinson

My mom is actually a former prima ballerina, and all the women in my family are associated either with dance or choreography or acting, so I'm very lucky in a way because I grew up in a family of artists. I've been dancing since I was a little kid.

Ksenia Solo

From the time I was 16 to really up until turning 21, the roles were really, really few and far between. I had people say that I just wasn't a good singer. They didn't know what to do with me; I would never fit in any markets. I almost quit acting altogether.

Naya Rivera

Some stars like to hide behind the whole idea of acting. But really good actors are not hiding at all. They're not afraid to be disliked, to be a little unsavoury.

Mary Elizabeth Mastrantonio

Sincerity and the correct use of the voice are the greatest things in the art of acting.

Alla Nazimova

I'm not the best actor I can be, so I'm just working on it. I'm not the quickest reader in the world but when I get an acting book I can read it in two days.

Evan Peters

It was a wonderful experience to work with Sylvia. She pushed me to be more powerful with my acting, and she told me scores of the most incredible stories I've ever heard. She is amazing.

Lukas Haas

I was working in customer service and had a verbally abusive boss. One day, I decided to quit and pursue my acting passion with everything I had. One week after quitting, I booked 'One Life to Live.'

Tika Sumpter

I put my friends and family first. I'm really just a normal thirteen-year-old girl who has a different hobby than most girls my age. Acting is kind of an extracurricular activity.

Natasha Calis

I grew up dancing my whole life, and I always kind of perceived that's what I would do professionally. But when I caught the acting bug, I knew I needed to go with no turning back.

Jacob Artist

Trust the acting.

Jean-Marc Vallee

Playing Karen was so satisfying that it almost cured my acting bug completely. Not that I had conquered the world of acting. It was just that I had something to prove to myself when I started Will & Grace. Now I feel like, okay, well, I've satisfied that.

Megan Mullally

I love all kinds of art. I mean, I love sketching and acting and music.

Amandla Stenberg

I remember going to acting class, so certain that no one's ever going to know my name.

Debby Ryan

Acting was something that I grew up just doing. I certainly never thought about it.

Gaby Hoffmann

I want the Israeli government to be made accountable for its behaviour to the Palestinians, and I want the people of the U.S. to cease acting as if they don't understand what is going on.

Alice Walker

I started missing acting when I was in school, and I realized after being in the business after however many years that I was really interested in film.

Gaby Hoffmann

I'd started acting as a child. But I wanted to see if it was something my true personality was interested in. I stepped away from offers when I took five years off to go to college. I've only really just decided to whole-heartedly embrace acting.

Gaby Hoffmann

I just love acting.

Joan Rivers

Acting is nothing more or less than playing. The idea is to humanize life.

George Eliot

I would rather miss the mark acting well than win the day acting basely.

Sophocles

Man is a make-believe animal: he is never so truly himself as when he is acting a part.

William Hazlitt

The real joy is in constructing a sentence. But I see myself as an actor first because writing is what you do when you are ready and acting is what you do when someone else is ready.

Steve Martin

Acting should be bigger than life. Scripts should be bigger than life. It should all be bigger than life.

Bette Davis

It is the habit of every aggressor nation to claim that it is acting on the defensive.

Jawaharlal Nehru

I have fun acting, and I want to do more of it, and I want to direct my own movie.

Demetri Martin

I don't get acting jobs because of my looks.

W. H. Auden

Acting in anger and hatred throughout my life, I frequently precipitated what I feared most, the loss of friendships and the need to rely upon the very people I'd abused.

Luke Ford

I took ballet dancing forever, and there was a natural transition into acting.

Judy Greer

My most useful acting tip came from my pal John Wayne. Talk low, talk slow, and don't say too much.

Michael Caine

Quite often in acting, you have to play a certain part; you cannot speak as much as you want to speak.

Sylvester Stallone

We've defined decency down now that we look at the entertainment value of it, whether the acting is good, the writing is good, the story is good, no matter the depravity, we'll watch it.

Rush Limbaugh

If Romney would go ideological in explaining Obama, it would help. We gotta stop the, 'He's a nice guy' stuff. Nice guys don't do what Obama is doing. Nice guys don't say and do and act the way Obama is saying, doing, and acting.

Rush Limbaugh

It's not just about acting. I love film, I'm a director now, I love writing, I love producing, I love having a company that makes films and to be prolific and have a place to put all the ideas that are constantly bubbling up inside of me and that don't let me sleep at night.

Drew Barrymore

People always ask me if I'm going to stop modeling because I have started an acting career. I hope to continue to model for years to come.

Tyra Banks

Great acting may be a turn-on, but it won't make me fantasize about the person for a week.

Sandra Bullock

To stay interested in acting, I have to keep trying stuff I've never done before.

Jessica Lange

It's fine to seek professional help, but I urge everyone - no matter how big their portfolio - to truly understand every suggestion they're given before acting.

Suze Orman

I think when you're acting, you usually don't have to know too much beyond how to pronounce the words you're saying.

Alan Alda

Acting is a life of rejection.

Lauren Bacall

I do this acting thing mostly for myself. I like to make a connection and communicate with the audience to make myself feel less lonely. I also do it to develop my own character, so sometimes I do it to just be away in a certain area that I've never been to. But mostly, the story has to do something for me.

Carice van Houten

When I started acting, there were parts in English that I thought I just had to try it out and go to another country. I did a film in Ireland. It was my first film abroad.

Carice van Houten

I've done some acting and a lot of different things, but mostly it's the music.

Joan Jett

Acting is a form of confession.

Tallulah Bankhead

What's interesting about the process of acting is how often you don't know what you're doing.

Alan Rickman

I still do my comedy and my performance stuff and my acting so it's not all-consuming. But I do find myself drawing more and more these days.

Billy Connolly

I studied acting in school and then, of course, couldn't get an acting job.

Denis Leary

It was always part of the plan to move into acting.

Aaliyah

My brother's my teacher, my mentor, and we both learnt all the acting basics from our father.

Jeff Bridges

No one should ever know where conduct ends and acting begins. Conduct unbecoming. That's what acting is.

Peter O'Toole

At the end of drama school, I made a contract with myself: I'd try acting for five years. I was 26. I had already spent eight years working in restaurants and gas stations. So I had seen enough small businesses to understand that that's what acting is: a small business.

Hugh Jackman

I'm acting when I serve as a hostess, when I run my wig business. I was born to act, and life itself is the greatest part.

Eva Gabor

If you do things, whether it's acting or music or painting, do it without fear - that's my philosophy. Because nobody can arrest you and put you in jail if you paint badly, so there's nothing to lose.

Anthony Hopkins

I hit the ground running, without a lot of training, so I had to do whatever I could do to survive as a professional, and if that meant being that character 24/7 and acting out, I was going to do that. I lived those characters, I brought them home with me.

Nicolas Cage

I'd done about 10 movies before I decided I wanted to make acting the main thrust of my career.

Jeff Bridges

I'd started going to acting classes at 14, played 'Medea' at 15 and really wanted to be a classical actress.

Barbra Streisand

You shouldn't have to give things up for someone. If you love them someone, you should love them for everything they do and all that they are. I love acting and I wouldn't give it up for anything, and I don't know anyone in my life who would ask me to give it up.

Lindsay Lohan

Acting can be so much fun that it's easy to forget that what you're doing is a job. But if I've got my tie on, I'm going to work.

Ashton Kutcher

You don't know when you're being watched. That's one of the weird things about celebrity. It's my least favorite part of acting, celebrity.

Denzel Washington

When I first started acting, I was just crap.

Heath Ledger

In acting, you have to pull from real-life situations, from people, to help develop a character.

Kevin Hart

I knew at an early age I wanted to act. Acting was always easy for me. I don't believe in predestination, but I do believe that once you get where ever it is you are going, that is where you were going to be.

Morgan Freeman

With proper acting, I don't know what I would play - I got sent a script for a play, and it said in the notes that my proposed character was 'hideously fat and ugly'. That made my day. I mean, I do know I am no oil painting.

Jo Brand

I love acting, but it's much more fun taking the kids to the zoo.

Nicole Kidman

What once was an expression of who I was - acting - also became my hiding place.

Salma Hayek

The ultimate goal is to change Syria's behaviour on a variety of issues - on its interference in Lebanese internal affairs, on its support for Palestinian terrorist groups that oppose the Palestinian Authority, on, most importantly, acting as a land bridge between Iran and Hezbollah, where Hezbollah gets all its arms.

Elliott Abrams

Acting is also working with people who invite you into their dreams and trust you with their innermost being.

Catherine Deneuve

I kind of fell backwards into acting. I was studying to be a high school teacher. I look now and I understand completely, or actually barely, how much work it is to be a teacher. It's an incredible amount of work.

Nathan Fillion

You need to become a good listener. As you're working, you hear someone else's lines and how you absorb them becomes your acting.

Jacqueline Bisset

You know, everyone says, 'Modeling and acting are so similar'... they say, 'It's so natural for models to become actresses because they use the camera.' I don't think of it in that way.

Gisele Bundchen

There's so much we can't express in our day-to-day interaction with people because it's considered inappropriate. And acting is all about being inappropriate.

Wentworth Miller

I wasn't really the most charming person, socially - it took me a long time to develop my people skills - but the one place I was always comfortable was onstage, acting or singing.

Zooey Deschanel

The actor cannot afford to look only to his own life for all his material nor pull strictly from his own experience to find his acting choices and feelings.

Stella Adler

An acting career usually has about a shelf life of ten years before people get sick of seeing you. It's a good thing to have a job to fall back on and I really do enjoy directing.

George Clooney

Movie acting suits me because I only need to be good for ninety seconds at a time.

Bill Murray

When I make a movie, I don't break it down and analyze it. I could but it would get in the way of doing a job - on instinct based on all the research we did going in. you want to trust yourself and your director and your acting partners in the circumstances you're shooting. I don't like to have any kind of overview.

Viggo Mortensen

And then, I suppose, there's also a cinematic reality on top of that. Because it was extremely difficult to keep tabs on, it was quite confusing acting that.

Gabriel Byrne

Most of my confidence came from being with ladies, because I certainly wasn't getting any acting jobs.

Vin Diesel

I grew up with horses when I was a kid in Argentina. I like them. I respect them. I'm careful around them. You never know what they're going to do. They're endlessly interesting. I've had some good acting partners that were horses over the years.

Viggo Mortensen

One of the nice things about acting is that it allows you to open up to the other people within you.

David Duchovny

Movie acting is about covering the machinery. Stage acting is about exposing the machinery. In cinema, you should think the actor is playing himself, if he's that good. It looks very easy. It should. But it's not, I assure you.

Michael Caine

I was a very extrovert kid. It felt normal to me to act. I always went to regular schools. I've never been catty or a prima donna, so I never had problems. I always had my seat at the cafeteria when I came back from acting.

Kirsten Dunst

The Tunisian blogger and activist Sami Ben Gharbia has written passionately about how U.S. government involvement in grassroots digital spaces can endanger those who are already vulnerable to accusations by nasty regimes of acting as foreign agents.

Rebecca MacKinnon

I probably wouldn't be acting if I didn't grow up in Hollywood.

Rashida Jones

At the risk of being forgotten completely by the media, I went to college and pursued a passion that had nothing to do with acting: mathematics.

Danica McKellar

Stand-up can take you in so many different places, man. So many doors can be opened up from stand-up comedy, and the first one that was opened up for me was acting. But you can go from acting to being a TV personality to being a radio personality to being a writer to being a producer, to just being a visionary, to voiceover work.

Kevin Hart

I got into acting because my teachers kept nudging me into it. The power a teacher has to influence someone is so great. I can't think of a profession I have more respect for.

Jon Hamm

With 'Taxi Driver,' I had this eureka moment. I realized that acting could be much more than what I had been doing. I had to build a character that wasn't me.

Jodie Foster

I'm getting positive feedback for my acting so we'll see if any other interesting parts come up.

Johnny Vegas

I think when you take away all, like, the premieres and press stuff and all the special effects, then you just come down to the fact that it's all about acting, and I think that has been the best bit for me.

Emma Watson

I have four to five months, tops, per year to give to my acting work.

Meryl Streep

When the target audience is American teenage kids, you can have problems. My generation prized really fine acting and writing. Sometimes you have to go back to the basic principles which underpin great visual comedy.

John Cleese

I never took acting classes, but I knew I could do it based on the skill with which I lied to my parents on a regular basis!

Ryan Reynolds

All I have to do is be me on stage. But acting, I have to be someone else, and walk how they would walk and blink how they would blink. I used to talk about it bad like, 'Aw man, that person made $10 million a movie?' But now I understand why they do. I get it now.

Jill Scott

Singing and acting suit me. I made a vow to myself to do everything that I can do with this life that I have, and I have to find the time to do this. Sometimes I need to be an actress. Sometimes I don't need to be Jill. However, everyone is always looking for the Jill in everything.

Jill Scott

To me, the stand up part in my life is great. I know I can do that. When I get an acting chance, I'm really thrilled.

Don Rickles

As much as we Egyptians treasure our military, acting alone it cannot provide the legitimacy to lay the foundations for democracy.

Mohamed ElBaradei

For me, acting is about getting away from myself. So to look at myself is the last thing I want.

Helena Bonham Carter

I love acting but I don't like all of the other stuff associated with it. The interest in celebrities, the press, the Internet, when your identity becomes mixed up in the way people are preceving you.

Nicole Kidman

Whenever I think of the high salaries we are paid as film actors, I think it is for the travel, the time away, and any trouble you get into through being well known. It's not for the acting, that's for sure.

Bill Murray

I don't know if acting is what I want to do for the rest of my life, it's just what I've, you know, ended up doing when I was little, and I've kinda grown up with it.

Natalie Portman

McCain is the kid who was really cool in middle school but never got high school game and people are sick of him acting like he's still popular.

Adam McKay

Corporations, consumers, and citizens must begin acting in concert to create a powerful third pillar of social transformation if we hope to meet the social challenges we currently face with equal force. This begins with corporations that choose to alter how they practice capitalism in two ways to serve the greater good.

Simon Mainwaring

I just want to bring as much natural as I can. I'm not saying that people who take acting lessons are false. They're much better than I am, but it doesn't work for me.

Betty White

They're called 'action scenes' because they do the acting for you. You don't have to act in action scenes. The action does it all for you. It's great.

Helen Mirren

I never really wanted to grow up. I grew up really young. I moved out when I was 13 - that's when I started acting.

Helena Bonham Carter

With acting, I didn't get much from it.

Karl Pilkington

I did a lot of acting at school and university, then I went to drama school. It was quite a normal route.

Benedict Cumberbatch

Actors walk around wearing these little tool-belts of acting skills. And I just don't find that interesting to watch. I never want to see someone who clearly can cry at the drop of a hat. That's so uninteresting.

Kristen Stewart

I would have given up acting in a minute. I didn't like how it set me apart from other people.

Jane Fonda

Acting is really about showing up that day and telling the writers what you feel like saying.

Tina Fey

I wanted to write plays. I was at Yale graduate school at the time for English literature, not for acting... I liked the idea of collaboration, and I thought if I'm gonna write plays, I should learn something about speaking the lines that I might try to write.

David Duchovny

Acting isn't that hard, really. I mean, I think that people make a big deal about it, but you just kind of try to say your lines naturally.

Ryan Gosling

I feel that one of the hardest things in acting is the way you need to switch your emotions.

Abhishek Bachchan

The good thing about acting is that it always keeps you on your toes... It's not like any other job where you can go in and do the same thing as yesterday.

Leonardo DiCaprio

I was aware that I was not getting the good acting roles because I was either too handsome, too pretty or whatever. I was being judged in ways that left me nowhere to go. You have to be patient.

Pierce Brosnan

In acting, there's a type of courage you're recognized for all the time. You lose 100 pounds and play a guy with AIDS, and you get rewarded. But, in life, doing what is courageous is quiet, and no one knows about it. Courage is someone making sacrifices for their family or making selfless decisions for what they hope or feel.

Rob Lowe

The sooner we put Egypt on the right track, the sooner we would be able to have an Egypt that is modern, that is moderate, and that is acting as a beacon for freedom and liberty across the Arab world.

Mohamed ElBaradei

I did a play called Throne of Straw when I was 11, at the Odyssey Theatre in Los Angeles. It became really clear to me at that point that I enjoyed acting more than any other experience I was having.

Kiefer Sutherland

Sigmund Freud said we act out our own dreams, but if you are only an actor you are not acting out your own dream. You are simply participating in someone else's dream.

John Malkovich

Whenever you have dynamic interactions between 300 million people and the American economy acting in really complex ways, that introduces a degree of almost chaos theory to the system, in a literal sense.

Nate Silver

We give antibiotics to people when they're dying or when they're not well; that's acting God. I mean, acting God is using the tools of creation to try and improve human life, human existence. I don't think that that's a huge problem.

Robert Winston

So I don't think I'm gonna pull my head into my shell just because a bunch of people start acting like idiots.

Todd Rundgren

I didn't get into acting to have a moment, I got into it because of people who've inspired me, like Judi Dench, Holly Hunter, and Jodie Foster.

Amy Adams

Acting with creatures that aren't there is kind like acting with an actor who refuses to come out of his trailer. You still have to go on and do the scene.

Liam Neeson

I try to be a hard boiled sometimes. My kids see right through it. I'm acting. It's always, 'When I say you'll be back at 11, that means 11, not 11.15. Do you hear me!?' Then, 'Yeah, Dad.'

Liam Neeson

Well, from an acting point of view, I bear no relation, I don't look like Alfred Kinsey at all, but I thought somewhere in my artist's soul, my actor's soul, I could capture something of the spirit of the man.

Liam Neeson

I love acting and making your own luck. You have to recreate yourself, I guess. Although, I don't know how.

Dennis Quaid

When you really get it right in acting, it's an act of empathy. You feel less distant from others, and that is really exciting.

Claire Danes

I feel like acting is something I've been working towards longer. And it would be great to win a Grammy, of course, but for some reason, an Oscar speaks more to me.

Vanessa Hudgens

The basic essential of a great actor is that he loves himself in acting.

Jessamyn West

At 23 it was all about acting. Today it's getting my kids to school, making sure that they've done their homework. I'm in my fifties, and I'm turning into a square.

Gary Oldman

The Chinese seemed to be mourning Mao in a heartfelt fashion. But I wondered how many of their tears were genuine. People had practiced acting to such a degree that they confused it with their true feelings.

Jung Chang

I learned a valuable lesson doing 'Mr. Sunshine,' which is that I didn't want to be in charge because it's too much. Being in charge and acting in every scene was just too difficult. It's like eating dinner in a moving golf cart every night.

Matthew Perry

I was really young, just playing with puppets a lot and doing all the voices and acting it out - normal kid stuff. But then I'd hear my mother talking about it to her relatives, marveling at it as if it was something unique. And it made me realize, 'Oh, maybe I do have a talent for something.'

Steve Buscemi

I was just doing bits and pieces of acting in the U.K. I'd been in the film 'Breaking and Entering' - Anthony Minghella gave me my start and I miss him dearly. Then I made the trip out to L.A., during one of their pilot seasons, which was when they were developing 'Gossip Girl,' and I auditioned, and things came together.

Ed Westwick

I was ashamed to admit I was hipped to the idea of acting. That's why I started in with the props.

John Wayne

I really enjoy singing, it's entirely different to acting because I'm just being myself.

Michelle Dockery

This is as true in everyday life as it is in battle: we are given one life and the decision is ours whether to wait for circumstances to make up our mind, or whether to act, and in acting, to live.

Omar N. Bradley

I enjoy acting when you really hit it right.

Marilyn Monroe

I just happened to step into acting. And now I can't imagine myself doing anything else.

Dylan O'Brien

The people of God want pastors, not clergy acting like bureaucrats or government officials.

Pope Francis

In my writing I am acting as a map maker, an explorer of psychic areas, a cosmonaut of inner space, and I see no point in exploring areas that have already been thoroughly surveyed.

William S. Burroughs

I know this may come as a shock to most of you, but I've decided to quit acting. I will not be auditioning for anything anymore, and if I get offered something like a role in a movie or a commercial or something, I will graciously turn it down. It's been great, but its just not for me anymore.

Chris Pratt

When in doubt, make a fool of yourself. There is a microscopically thin line between being brilliantly creative and acting like the most gigantic idiot on earth. So what the hell, leap.

Cynthia Heimel

Acting is a very personal process. It has to do with expressing your own personality, and discovering the character you're playing through your own experience - so we're all different.

Ian Mckellen

When an actor plays a scene exactly the way a director orders, it isn't acting. It's following instructions. Anyone with the physical qualifications can do that.

James Dean

I'm going to write a book, continue acting, continue motivational speaking and just share with people who I am and what I've learned in my second chance of life and pass it on to people in their first chance of life.

J. R. Martinez

Listen, acting is not surgery, it's entertainment. You're doing something to hopefully move people, to make them laugh, to transport them. But actors are vulnerable, and the reason we're vulnerable is that we're always trying to recreate human behaviour.

Eddie Redmayne

Acting is a nice childish profession - pretending you're someone else and, at the same time, selling yourself.

Katharine Hepburn

The only time I commit to conspiracy theories is when something way retarded happens. Like Lee Harvey Oswald acting alone.

Joe Rogan

When I went to Los Angeles right after high school, I got some acting jobs, and I never, ever wanted to be an actress! Public speaking and acting make me want to vomit. But I have never been nervous singing. When it comes to public speaking, I stumble on my words, sweat, and pull at my clothes.

Kelly Clarkson

Acting never was about the money for me... Maybe in 10 years, I'll be able to appreciate the fact that I am financially stable and independent and I don't have to make bad choices. I can be very picky.

Emma Watson

I remember acting in a school play about the melting pot when I was very little. There was a great big pot onstage. On the other side of the pot was a little girl who had dark hair, and she and I were representing the Italians. And I thought: Is that what an Italian looked like?

Al Pacino

When I was in high school, I was a bad singer. I mean, all my early acting was musical theater, and my first ever show was 'Jesus Christ Superstar.' Everyone's familiar with it. I played priest number 3 and sang so out of tune that it's not even funny.

Sam Claflin

Of course, when I say that human nature is gentleness, it is not 100 percent so. Every human being has that nature, but there are many people acting against their nature, being false.

Dalai Lama

Acting is the greatest answer to my loneliness that I have found.

Claire Danes

When I decided that I might want to do acting for a living - I don't know where it really came from, since there was no school play or any of that - my mom gave me her blessing. I had to get a scholarship - that was the only way I could have gone to drama school.

Gary Oldman

Acting is fun for me and it doesn't really matter how, whether it's hard work or easy work, it's always fun.

Tommy Lee Jones

I have a fine level of recognition in the business and among the acting community now, so I consider myself one of the lucky ones. If I didn't think that, there would be something wrong with me. I'm grateful and thankful for what I've got.

Philip Seymour Hoffman

There is a part of your brain that has to stop when you're acting. You have to be in the moment and dare to fly. Words can't be on your mind.

Penelope Cruz

I'm addicted to Altoids. I call them 'acting pills.'

Harrison Ford

I remember once acting really cool on a bus with this girl named Stephanie. When I got home, I realized that I had a really big zit on my forehead. If you have acne problems, you really shouldn't be acting like Don Juan. I should have been contrite - and apologized for exposing her to the angry pimple.

John Cusack

With acting, you wanna see if you can get into trouble without knowing how you're gonna get out of it. It's like the exact opposite of war, where you need an exit strategy. When you're acting, you should get all the way into trouble with no exit strategy, and have the cameras rolling.

John Cusack

It's true; I have a skill and it's... it has not related to acting, it's not related to auditions, it's not related to studios, not related to public whim. It's whether I'm funny or not and whether I can entertain people.

Tim Allen

Whether it's acting, directing or writing, I want to be involved in the film industry for the rest of my life.

Tom Felton

I took a break from acting for four years to get a degree in mathematics at UCLA, and during that time I had the rare opportunity to actually do research as an undergraduate. And myself and two other people co-authored a new theorem: Percolation and Gibbs States Multiplicity for Ferromagnetic Ashkin-Teller Models on Two Dimensions, or Z2.

Danica McKellar

Caregiving requires the intention of love, caretaking requires the intention of fear. Not acting in anger when you are angry requires the intention of love.

Gary Zukav

I have a lot of great distractions outside of acting.

Heath Ledger

I was raised in New York City and raised in the New York City theater world. My father was a theater director and an acting teacher, and it was not uncommon for me to have long discussions about the method and what the various different processes were to finding a character and exploring character and realizing that character.

Vin Diesel

When I'm acting, I'm in a different place, singing is the last thing on my mind, and when I'm on stage, there's no acting at all involved, not even presentation, it's just who I am.

Harry Connick, Jr.

Acting forces me to socialise, which is good for me, I think.

Jesse Eisenberg

I'm not a Method actor. I don't believe acting should be psychodrama. I look within myself and see what I can find to play the role with. If I'm playing a blind man, I don't go around blindfolded for days. A lot of good actors would, but I don't go in for that very much. I like to just make it up as I go along.

John Malkovich

A lot of what acting is paying attention.

Nancy Reagan

In dance you use every party of your body except your voice. I wanted to start acting because I wanted to use my voice.

Zoe Saldana

I am not deeply involved in Australian politics but I know there are prime ministers, governments around the world who are not acting responsibly in relation to climate change.

Jane Goodall

If my mum thinks I'm acting like a diva she'll soon tell me off... She'll cut me down to size!

Katherine Jenkins

Acting for me is very therapeutic. It's my shrink.

Taraji P. Henson

Sitting at the table during Color Purple and looking up and suddenly realizing I was acting in front of Steven Spielberg, was pretty cool. It was pretty good.

Whoopi Goldberg

My movies are unadorned, they're not particularly fancy, I think they're kind of workmanlike in some ways, focusing on the writing and the acting.

Ben Affleck

I think the beauty of working with young people is they remind you of the spirit of acting and it's just a big play.

Eric Bana

I love acting like I'm in love. It's a very positive thing.

Amanda Seyfried

In those days, reserve duty lasted for six years, which, I might add, was three times as long as service in the regular army, although to be perfectly honest, I was unable to fulfill my entire obligation because I was taking acting classes and they said I could skip my last year.

Larry David

Acting is an art form and you want to take roles that are challenged and it's more of a challenge I think to play dark characters. Not that I want to always play those, but it is a challenge and challenges are rewarding and fun.

James Franco

When you're modeling you're actually acting for the camera and the photographer. It's more fun, too because there are no lines to memorize.

Cindy Margolis

I don't know if this is why everything has worked so well and I'm not sure I'd recommend this kind of thinking to anyone else, but I've always known I'd be successful in acting. I have certainly worked for it.

Jennifer Lawrence

When we say gender is performed, we usually mean that we've taken on a role or we're acting in some way and that our acting or our role playing is crucial to the gender that we are and the gender that we present to the world.

Judith Butler

When I was a kid, I wanted to be serious, like Daniel Day-Lewis. No one really dreams of being a comic actor, do they? Now I realise how stupid that is - and it's because comic acting isn't taken seriously enough. It's a discipline. You know instantly - either you're funny and getting the laughs, or you're not.

Chris O'Dowd

Acting is all about honesty. If you can fake that, you've got it made.

George Burns

Why do we go around acting as though everything was friendship and reliability when basically everything everywhere is full of sudden hate and ugliness?

Anna Freud

A man of knowledge lives by acting, not by thinking about acting.

Carlos Castaneda

Acting is like a Halloween mask that you put on.

River Phoenix

I'm not a photographer, so I didn't get into F-stops or ND filters or background, foreground, cross-light, all that stuff. But I was interested in the camera and the lenses. That's the world that I'm moving in, in terms of acting and giving a performance.

Keanu Reeves

You know the circus performer who spins the plates in the air you know, and he'll spin six or seven plates in the air? Acting sometimes is kind of that guy spinning all those plates in the air but in your head and in your body.

Philip Seymour Hoffman

Bad acting comes in many bags, various odors. It can be performed by cardboard refugees from an Ed Wood movie, reciting their dialogue off an eye chart, or by hopped-up pros looking to punch a hole through the fourth wall from pure ballistic force of personality, like Joe Pesci in a bad mood. I can respect bad acting that owns its own style.

James Wolcott

Botox should be banned for actors, as steroids are for sportsmen. Acting is all about expression; why would you want to iron out a frown?

Rachel Weisz

Acting is just playing the violin in an orchestra. Directing is being the conductor.

Jason Bateman

Animation is a fascinating area from an acting point of view because it's not really like anything else because you are only providing a portion of the performance. That's very inspiring and it forces you to do things in a different way - to tell stories through your voice.

David Tennant

Acting isn't something you do. Instead of doing it, it occurs. If you're going to start with logic, you might as well give up. You can have conscious preparation, but you have unconscious results.

Lee Strasberg

It's important for me to be free and know I'm acting for myself. I do things because I want to, and that's important. You want to be your own person.

Stephenie Meyer

Acting is so much about waiting... waiting for an audition, waiting for the right part to come along. It's nice to write your own thing, write about what you're feeling and then go out and perform them. It's a nice thing to have and not get bored.

Emily Kinney

I left school and couldn't find acting work, so I started going to clubs where you could do stand-up. I've always improvised, and stand-up was this great release. All of a sudden, it was just me and the audience.

Robin Williams

I'm too busy acting like I'm not Naive. I've seen it all, I was here first.

Kurt Cobain

I have to work extra hard because I am dyslexic. People said that I couldn't be an actress, but I'm proving them wrong. Acting has helped me overcome the challenge.

Bella Thorne

Acting is my true love. I would like to have been a serious actor, and I plan to in the next life. I'm gonna be Meryl Streep Rivers.

Joan Rivers

Acting is happy agony.

Jean-Paul Sartre

To me, acting is the most logical way for people's neuroses to manifest themselves, in this great need we all have to express ourselves.

James Dean

The most important thing in acting is honesty. If you can fake that, you've got it made.

George Burns

I can do everything with ease on the stage, whereas in real life I feel too big and clumsy. So I didn't choose acting. It chose me.

Ingrid Bergman

If you took acting away from me, I'd stop breathing.

Ingrid Bergman

Acting means living, it's all I do and all I'm good at. If I weren't getting paid well, I would still be acting in a small troupe somewhere.

Morgan Freeman

With any role, you're extending yourself and acting out things that never happened to you.

Tom Hiddleston

One of the things about acting is it allows you to live other people's lives without having to pay the price.

Robert De Niro

I've honestly been really lucky. My only jobs have been babysitting and acting.

Anne Hathaway

I went to public school my whole life, graduated high school with my class. Growing up, I'd go to an audition, my friends would go to soccer practice and we'd all reconvene and hang out in our neighborhood. When I would book something, I would never tell my friends. Acting was just fun. I was a kid, I wasn't jaded.

Shailene Woodley

As always, with acting, you can't be too self-conscious. You shouldn't care about what people are thinking about you at the time because they're not caring about you, they're caring about the character.

Freddie Highmore

True freedom is the capacity for acting according to one's true character, to be altogether one's self, to be self-determined and not subject to outside coercion.

Corliss Lamont

You know, my parents have always been incredibly supportive. I'm an only child, so we're very close. There's just the three of us. They're exceptional parents but also great friends. My father was able to take his hobby, photography, and turn it into a beautiful career. So when they saw how much I loved acting, they were 100 percent behind me.

Sophia Bush

For me, acting is about the art of it and it's about being on a film set and doing your thing, painting a blank canvas.

Shailene Woodley

I was kind of scared of failing at acting.

James Franco

I find acting tough, but sitting around chatting - that's easy.

Nick Frost

I'm going to try to not let anyone put me in a box, and that certainly applies to the things I do outside of acting.

James Franco

Acting isn't really a creative profession. It's an interpretative one.

Paul Newman

If all the circumstances of acting are made to easy, then there's no grain of sand to make the pearl.

Peter Sarsgaard

Comedy was why I got into acting the first place. Peter Sellers was a huge influence on my wanting to act. I grew up with him and found him hysterical. The Pink Panther films were an inspiration, from my earliest childhood days, when I was watching them with my brother and my dad.

Sally Hawkins

I love acting. But I love being a mother. To be a full mother and a full person, you have to do what you love, and that's acting. But I like the best of both worlds.

Tracey Gold

I had given thought to acting, but I never really had a good enough opportunity or a character who made sense and paralleled my life a little bit. I feel like I'm one of the poster boys for a bad guy in a movie. I feel like I'm a good person to play a bad guy in a movie. I can say that.

Gucci Mane

It stands to the everlasting credit of science that by acting on the human mind it has overcome man's insecurity before himself and before nature.

Albert Einstein

When I went home from Juilliard, I couldn't find acting work.

Robin Williams

Two young actresses I admire are Emma Stone and Emma Watson, because they are intelligent, talented actresses and have a great sense of humor. They have learned to balance what they love in life -

acting, school and everything else.

Kara Hayward

Every man has inside himself a parasitic being who is acting not at all to his advantage.

William S. Burroughs

I was planning to go into architecture. But when I arrived, architecture was filled up. Acting was right next to it, so I signed up for acting instead.

Gilbert K. Chesterton

I am acquainted with no immaterial sensuality so delightful as good acting.

Lord Byron

A multitude of causes unknown to former times are now acting with a combined force to blunt the discriminating powers of the mind, and unfitting it for all voluntary exertion to reduce it to a state of almost savage torpor.

William Wordsworth

Everything is acting.

Marilyn Manson

More than in any other performing arts the lack of respect for acting seems to spring from the fact that every layman considers himself a valid critic.

Simone Weil

One of the things I love about acting is that it reveals a certain something about yourself, but it doesn't reveal your own personal story.

Jessica Lange

Acting deals with very delicate emotions. It is not putting up a mask. Each time an actor acts he does not hide; he exposes himself.

Jeanne Moreau

All of us should have free choice when it comes to patriotic displays... a government wisely acting within its bounds will earn loyalty and respect from its citizens. A government dare not demand the same.

Jesse Ventura

Acting has given me a way to channel my angst. I feel like an overweight, pimply faced kid a lot of the time - and finding a way to access that insecurity, and put it toward something creative is incredibly rewarding. I feel very lucky.

Ryan Reynolds

Acting is always at the core of my life, but I'm also excited about producing. I'm excited about directing, and I have a life in the filmmaking world, and so I want to explore all aspects of it, not just the acting, but acting is the root.

Nicolas Cage

Begin within. If it shows up in your life, it's coming to tell you something about you that you're acting like you don't know. Something about yourself, or your relationship with God.

Iyanla Vanzant

I'm just starting to scratch the surface of what really makes me happy and it's taken me a while to admit that acting like a little child and being a jerk and a punk is fun.

Leonardo DiCaprio

Psychology and acting are very closely linked. It's just about studying people and how they work. It can be an incredible discipline and exercise.

Claire Danes

The best thing about acting is that I get to lose myself in another character and actually get paid for it... It's a great outlet. I'm not really sure who I am - it seems I change every day.

Leonardo DiCaprio

Acting is not an important job in the scheme of things. Plumbing is.

Spencer Tracy

Acting on a good idea is better than just having a good idea.

Robert Half

I think I'm an actor because I have very strong imagination and empathy. I never studied acting, but those two qualities are exactly the qualities that make for an activist.

Susan Sarandon

Acting is the most personal of our crafts. The make-up of a human being - his physical, mental and emotional habits - influence his acting to a much greater extent than commonly recognized.

Lee Strasberg

I like the character roles. Somewhere back there I really came to the conclusion in my mind that the difference between acting and stardom was major. And that if you become a star, people are going to go to see you. If you remain an actor, they're going to go and see the story you're in.

Morgan Freeman

It would be easy to say that I want to play a role that was very much like myself, but more or less with acting, you get to be all these different things, and you aren't trying to be yourself, so it's escapism in a way.

Summer Altice

Marriage requires a special talent, like acting. Monogamy requires genius.

Warren Beatty

When you're young, you don't really know quite what you're aiming at. You're very impulsive and acting on impulse, which is very important and valuable. But you're kind of swimming in a blind sea. When you get older, you have more of a sense of direction.

Sinead O'Connor

Science is not a heartless pursuit of objective information. It is a creative human activity, its geniuses acting more as artists than as information processors.

Stephen Jay Gould

The reason why I found acting is because my father passed away. He passed away really young. I was going to go to med school. My father's dream was that all of his kids become doctors. I realized in school I didn't like it. When he died, it was like a wake-up call. Life is too short to do something you don't want to do.

Adepero Oduye

I'm in the acting business. That's the ego business.

Betty White

I never wanted to be a model. My modelling career was nothing but a stepping stone to my acting career and that's all I ever saw it as. A pointless rock in the river that has to be stepped on in order to get to the meaningful oasis of acting.

Halle Berry

Acting is like peeling an onion. You have to peel away each layer to reveal another.

Juliette Binoche

Storytelling is my currency. It's my only worth. The only thing of value I have in this life is my ability to tell a story, whether in print, orating, writing it down or having people acting it out.

Kevin Smith

'

When I was 16, I played Macbeth at school and my English teacher said, 'I think you may have acting talent. Try to get into the National Youth Theatre of Great Britain and see where you get.' I wouldn't have thought of that at all. I wanted to be a surgeon, but I wasn't a clever man.

David Suchet

I got into acting my junior year of high school. We got a new hot drama teacher and I was like 'Alright, I'll try drama.'

Miles Teller

To me acting is like a jigsaw puzzle. The jigsaw puzzle is of the sky and all the pieces are blue. Out of this you have to create a human being and put it together.

Henry Winkler

As human beings, we aren't as individual as we'd like to believe we are. And I think that's what makes acting possible. Despite the fact that I have not experienced something, I have it in my human capacity to imagine it and to put myself in someone else's shoes, and to take someone else's circumstances personally.

Lupita Nyong'o

All companies of any size have to continue to push to make sure you get the right leaders, the right team, the right people to be fast acting, and fast moving in the marketplace. We've got great leaders, and we continue to attract and promote great new leaders.

Steve Ballmer

Acting is not about anything romantic, not even fantasy, although you do create fantasy.

James Earl Jones

Acting is experience with something sweet behind it.

Humphrey Bogart

Communication between band-mates is imperative. Communication is the key to any healthy relationship. If I need to be checked, I expect to hear it put in plain words what my faults are, and give my band-mates the ultimate consideration by shutting up and listening, then acting on the advice given. Same goes for anyone else in any band.

Phil Anselmo

Acting, to me, is about the incredible adventure of examining the landscape of human heart and soul. That's basically what we do.

Glenn Close

I love acting. It's my playground, it let's me explore. But my happiness in this world - my level of peace - is never going to be dictated by acting.

Chris Evans

The thing I like a lot about acting is I'll never learn enough. I'll never know it inside and out.

Dylan O'Brien

All these fifty-year-old guys wearing baseball caps and shorts and acting like children. It winds me up. Men don't have to take responsibility anymore. Most of the guys I know would punch me on the nose for saying this, but maybe we do have to bring back conscription.

Chrissie Hynde

Whatever it is, if you draw, you paint, you're a carpenter, you play football, the more you do it, you're a journalist, the more stories you write, the more people you interview and navigate your way through these different personalities to get your story, the better you're going to get at it. Acting's no different.

Tom Sizemore

Acting isn't for me. I don't like being told what to do. I'm more interested in set design, more visually driven.

Sofia Coppola

There are two main jobs in acting - the first one is to be a good actor, and the second one is to convince everyone that you're a good actor.

Laurence Fox

I would like to be known as an 'artist'. Whether that be music, acting, sketching, cooking, whatever. I'm interested in all of those things.

Mark Salling

Acting is a freelance career... you never stop having to prove yourself and fight for work.

Miranda Otto

I would never butt heads with Rob Zombie. I don't know anybody that's in acting that ever butted heads with Rob Zombie. I adore Rob. I adore him. I adore working with him. I adore knowing him. I'm happy to consider myself a friend and someone who he hires. I just think he's great.

Dee Wallace

Acting is my passion, and Chelsea FC is my hobby.

Phil Daniels

For an entire populace, change, growth, and spontaneity were dangerous. Acting upon a personal desire, whispering a hidden longing, revealing your true feelings - all the human actions we think of as essential to a character - had be censored by the self lest they be punished by the state.

Adam Johnson

Acting had been a hobby that turned into a career, the directing was a hobby that turned into a career and music just really allowed me to find another way to express myself.

Malcolm-Jamal Warner

If I had any advice for my 16-year-old self, it would just be to stay strong, because acting is not an easy lifestyle, especially when you are starting out. That being said, it definitely makes it all worth it when it does happen.

Melissa Benoist

The negative about acting is that you have to spend a great deal of time away from your friends and loved ones, but it's not like working a 9-5 job and only having two or three weeks off a year. I may not have seen my girlfriend for two or three months, but then we can spend two or three months together solidly.

Douglas Booth

The instinct of self-preservation in human society, acting almost subconsciously, as do all drives in the human mind, is rebelling against the constantly refined methods of annihilation and against the destruction of humanity.

Bertha von Suttner

At the end of the day, acting is all about telling lies. We are professional imposters and the audience accept that. We've made this deal that we tell you a tale and a pack of lies, but there will be a truth in it. You may enjoy it, or it will disturb you.

Pete Postlethwaite

Acting isn't a side thing - you have to live and breathe it.

Bella Thorne

I think probably the reason why I really enjoy acting is that I really am interested in people. I'm interested in what they think, why they think it and what happened in their lives to make them see things a certain way.

Maddie Hasson

Men acquire a particular quality by constantly acting in a particular way.

Aristotle

Every success story has a parent who says, 'over my dead body.' Every success story has an old person who walks up to you and says, when you're acting the fool, 'you know I worry about you sometimes.'

Bill Cosby

The art of acting consists in keeping people from coughing.

Benjamin Franklin

Being Michael Jordan means acting the same as I always have.

Michael Jordan

T.V. acting is a great skill to have, and it's nice to have that stability.

Debby Ryan

I love to continue acting. It's my passion.

Britt Robertson

Usually in a battle sequence when a bomb is going off, you forget you're acting.

Charlie Sheen

No passion so effectually robs the mind of all its powers of acting and reasoning as fear.

Edmund Burke

Acting is different from stand-up. It gives you this ability to enter into another character, to create another person.

Robin Williams

I want in 40 years to still be acting and to more than anything have longevity and not just be this huge flash in the pan and then disappear.

Debby Ryan

Going into my 20s, I was uncertain, trying to figure out what my relationship to acting is.

Gaby Hoffmann

I would definitely love to continue acting, and I also really enjoy school, so I would like to balance the two somehow.

Kara Hayward

I'm a history nerd. Actually acting's the best job for somebody who loves weird, different stuff.

Lauren Cohan

The political machine triumphs because it is a united minority acting against a divided majority.

Will Durant

Acting and the industry of making movies is beautiful, but it's so exhausting and such hard work; if you don't absolutely 100% want to do something, it defeats the purpose.

Debby Ryan

Acting is the perfect idiot's profession.

Katharine Hepburn

I would say that Emma Stone and Emma Watson are two very talented young actresses who are very intelligent and have a great sense of humor and have learned to balance what they love with their acting career, and I think that's really a great thing.

Kara Hayward

Everyone forgets comedians are actors. There's no question about it. A Robin Williams cannot say the same line every night for 40 weeks and make it sound fresh unless he's doing an acting job.

Joan Rivers

Acting is the most minor of gifts. After all, Shirley Temple could do it when she was four.

Katharine Hepburn

If you're saying the same line 10 times and making it look like you just came up with it, that's acting.

Joan Rivers

Acting is a question of absorbing other people's personalities and adding some of your own experience.

Jean-Paul Sartre